ETHNIC COSTUME

*Clothing Designs and Techniques
with an International Inspiration*

Lois Ericson and Diane Ericson

Illustrated by Diane Ericson

VNR **VAN NOSTRAND REINHOLD COMPANY**
New York Cincinnati Toronto London Melbourne

Printed in the United States of America
Designed by Loudan Enterprises

Published in 1979 by Van Nostrand Reinhold Company
A division of Litton Educational Publishing, Inc.
135 West 50th Street, New York, N.Y. 10020, U.S.A.

Van Nostrand Reinhold Limited
1410 Birchmount Road, Scarborough, Ontario M1P 2E7,
Canada

Van Nostrand Reinhold Australia Pty. Limited
17 Queen Street, Mitcham, Victoria 3132, Australia

Van Nostrand Reinhold Company Limited
Molly Millars Lane, Wokingham, Berkshire, England

16 15 14 13 12 11 10 9 8 7 6 5 4 3 2 1

Library of Congress Cataloging in Publication Data

Ericson, Diane.
  Ethnic costume.

  Bibliography: p.
  Includes index.
  1. Costume. I. Ericson, Lois, joint author.
II. Title.
TT633.E74   646.4'7   78-26062
ISBN 0-442-26781-9

To Lennart and Chas, our two best friends

Acknowledgments

We want to thank all the artist/
designers who so generously
shared their talents with us.

We wish them joy and satisfaction
in their future work.

A special thank-you to Lennart,
for his encouragement and preliminary editing.

CONTENTS

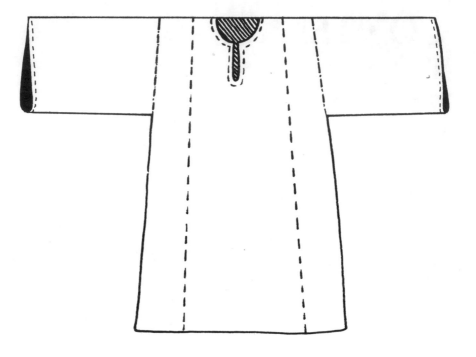

tu·nic (tōō′nik, tyōō′-), *n.* **1.** *Chiefly Brit.* a coat worn as part of a military or other uniform. **2.** a gownlike outer garment, with or without sleeves and sometimes belted, worn by the ancient Greeks and Romans. **3.** a woman's upper garment, either loose or close-fitting and extending over the skirt to the hips or below. **4.** a garment with a short skirt, worn by women for sports. **5.** *Eccles.* a tunicle. **6.** *Anat., Zool.* any covering or investing membrane or part, as of an organ. **7.** *Bot.* a natural integument. [OE *tunice* (occurs in acc. case *tunican*) < L *tunica*]

INTRODUCTION

In historical terms the primary considerations in the construction of clothing were the availability and width of the materials and the ease of movement for the wearer. In each culture the basic designs were similar for all social classes, with distinctions apparent in fabric and decoration.

In all periods of history people have worn some form of the tunic. "Tunic" is a universally used term, but it has many synonyms—*gallabia* in Egypt, *jubbah* in Turkey, *mashlah* in Israel, and *mente* in Hungary, to mention only a few. Its many forms have inspired the adaptations shown here.

With the wide selection of fabrics and prices available today, anyone can create and enjoy an aesthetic wardrobe. In the following pages many artists share their expertise, their spontaneity, and their originality with you. We invite you to explore with us the many possibilities of the tunic.

To directly apply the ideas for garments presented in this book, we suggest using similar styles of commercial patterns. These patterns offer a wide range of styles and are easily adaptable with few changes. If you are involved in pattern drafting, making your own patterns will be a simple matter. In either case we hope you enjoy meeting the challenge presented. Books on costume (see bibliography) are listed for additional inspiration and are a rich source of ideas.

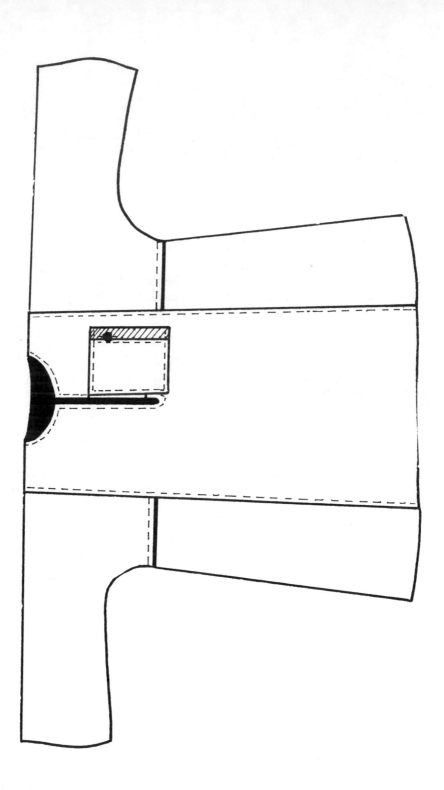

CHAPTER I.

The Shirt

The first commercial pattern appeared in 1860. It was a shirt designed by Ebenezer and Ellen Butterick.

1. Norway

Norwegian seamen wore very warm pullover shirts on their fishing expeditions in the North Sea. This style was popular for decades; it was made of very tightly woven dark blue wool. The plain tunic had long sleeves and a square neck with a rolled collar.

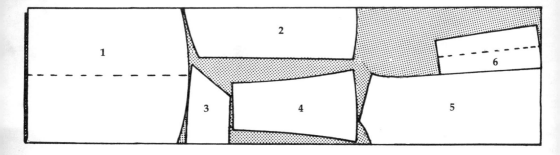

1 sleeve   2 side front   3 collar   4 front   5 back   6 side back

This blue pullover tunic is an adaptation of a simple peasant smock. The style was chosen to utilize a square piece of embroidered, handwoven, or appliquéd fabric as the main focus. In this case a red, white, and blue mola was used in the front panel. Small silver bells, coins, and animal figures dangle from several strands of perle cotton attached below the insert. The fabrics are cotton prints and lightweight handwoven materials.

Designer/photographer. Joanne Purpus, model: Leslie Suzuki

2. North Africa

This loose-fitting shirt with wide sleeves is called a *parasia* and was worn by well-to-do people in Morocco, North Africa. It is made of gauzelike cotton material and was usually worn belted over a caftan. The most popular colors for this garment were brown, wine red, dull green, and light blue. The belt was made of woolen cords from which were suspended various small weapons.

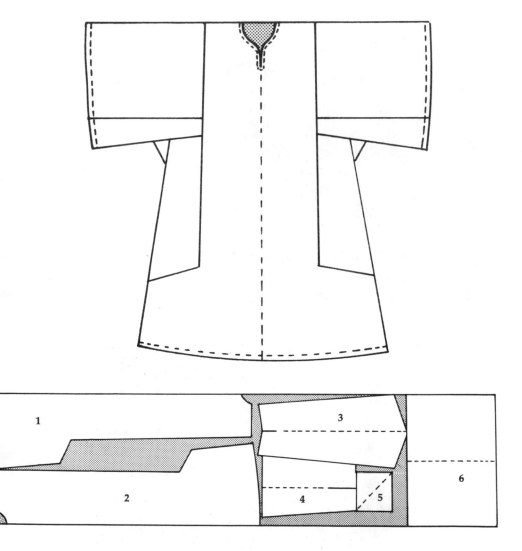

1 back   2 front   3 side piece   4 undersleeve   5 gusset   6 upper sleeve

The North African shirt influenced the cut of this tunic. Two different prints, both with butterfly designs, are coordinated with a black-and-white floral print. The butterfly prints are in warm colors—yellow, red, and orange. The ribbons that cover the raw edges of the appliqué and accentuate the lines are also in warm colors plus blue. The plain side panels are black. The hexagonal inset in the front is lightly padded and quilted to emphasize the designs.

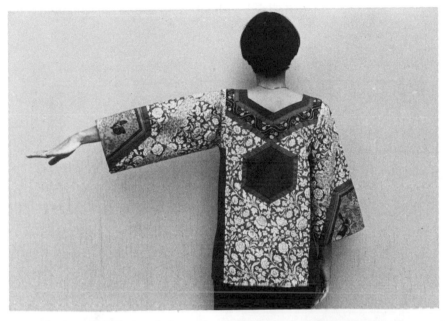

Designer/model: Annabel Woodsmall, photographer: Roger Woodsmall

3. Rumania

Many elegantly embroidered and handworked textiles come from Rumania. The cut of the garments was fairly simple, but the fine stitching made them prized possessions. With this shirt men wore fancy lambskin vests, pants that were shirred up the legs, and hand-made boots. A fur hat trimmed with ribbons and beads completed the colorful costume.

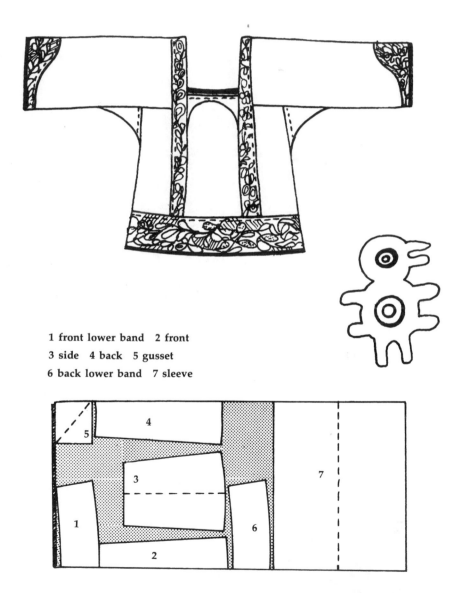

1 front lower band   2 front
3 side   4 back   5 gusset
6 back lower band   7 sleeve

This design motif is inspired by the 19th-century San Blas Indian technique of reverse appliqué. Teal blue and fuchsia are the colors of the 100%-cotton fabrics, which combine very effectively with ikat-dyed cotton in this "talking bird tunic." (The reverse-appliqué technique is described in chapter 6.)

Designer/model:
Alix Peshette,
photographer:
Libby Harmor

4. Finland

This man's jacket from Finland is made of a very heavy diagonally woven woolen fabric. The natural-colored garment is trimmed with yellow, red, and green woolen cord on the front and bands of the sleeves. The small appliqués on the sides and the lower part of the front panel are made of embroidered leather.

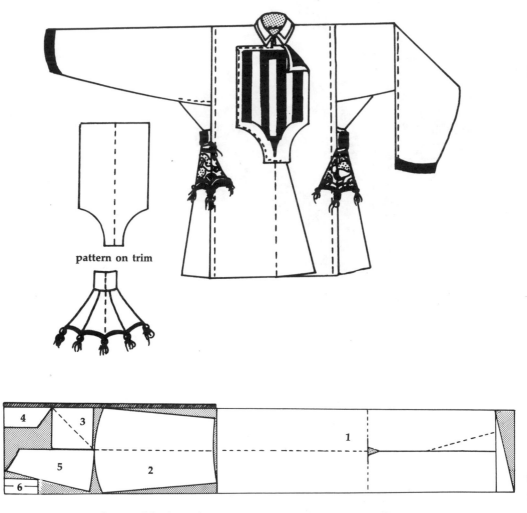

pattern on trim

1 front and back   2 sleeve   3 gusset   4 collar   5 side piece   6 cuffs

The design on this shirt depicts an endangered species. The eagles are in red with bright yellow talons and are appliquéd to a beige cotton fabric. Feather stitches (how appropriate!) outline some of the pieces. Silver-gray french knots accentuate the dark blue sections. Yellow and magenta bias strips finish the sleeve and neck edges.

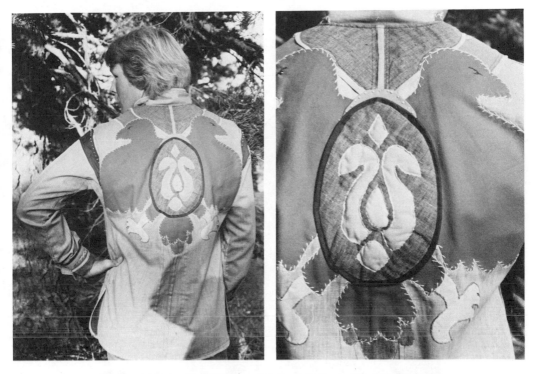

Designer/photographer: Diane Ericson Frode, model: Mike Ericson

This shirt, made of gray cotton, has a black yoke and cuffs piped with red satin. The strip appliqués are in red and cream satin and in red, gray, beige, and black cotton. The back inset is Seminole patchwork, a method of piecing and restitching fabric into interesting designs described in chapter 6. These shirts were both made from the same pattern, varying the collar slightly.

5. *Russia*

This shirt is typical of the tribes of the Caspian Steppes in Russia. The simple cut was used in many countries with slight variations. The plain fabric was usually silk or taffeta. To conserve these costly materials, flowered cottons were used in the sections that were covered by the jacket, which was made of velvet and decorated with gold braid and enameled ornaments. The cut of the outer garment was very similar to that of the shirt..

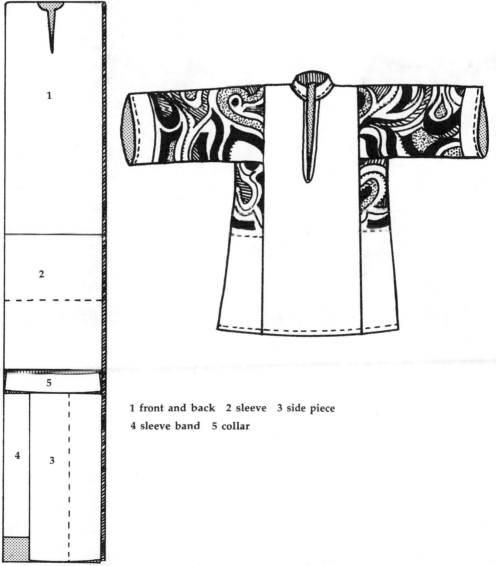

1 front and back   2 sleeve   3 side piece
4 sleeve band   5 collar

Tie-dyeing an old sheet in shades of pink, mauve, and navy was the first step in creating this shirt. The pattern pieces for the tunic were cut out of dark blue cotton. The tie-dyed sections were then appliquéd to the cotton by hand. The slits on the side were faced to the outside to form pockets. The overall design of the shirt was based on the Japanese principle of *notan*, the balancing of black and white. The symbol appliquéd on the front continues this concept.

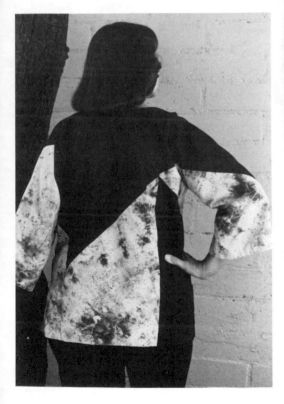

Designer/model: Jean Hudson, photographer: Jo Dendel

6. Norway

This wool shirt or blouse, worn by Nordic seamen, evolved from early Bronze Age garments. The insert at the shoulder and the long sleeves were added to a plain tunic. This Germanic style was adopted by working people all over Europe and is still in use today.

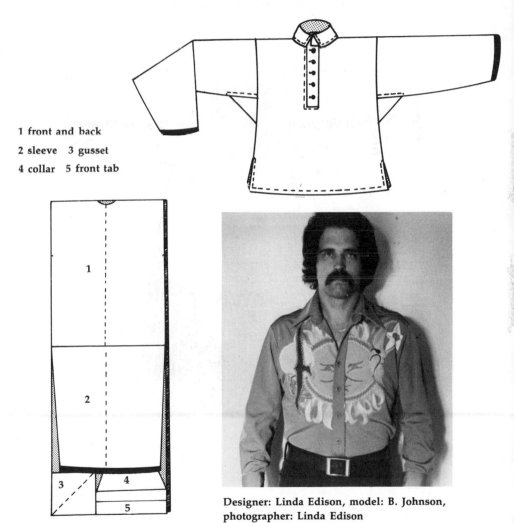

1 front and back
2 sleeve   3 gusset
4 collar   5 front tab

Designer: Linda Edison, model: B. Johnson, photographer: Linda Edison

The sun has been a popular motif for centuries, a symbol with many meanings—power, hope, rebirth, among others. This gold and orange sun is embroidered on a medium-blue polyester-knit shirt. This tunic has buttoned cuffs, collar, and front tab.

7. Macedonia

This woman's shirt from Macedonia is made of heavy, dense cotton and is embroidered with red and purple yarn. The neck edge and lower hems are lavishly ornamented with black braid, glass beads, and a red cord, which is used to attach small metal rings. The sleeve hems are faced with red fabric and decorated with cord and paillettes, which make them very firm. On top of this long shirt a felted vest and a fancy apron were worn.

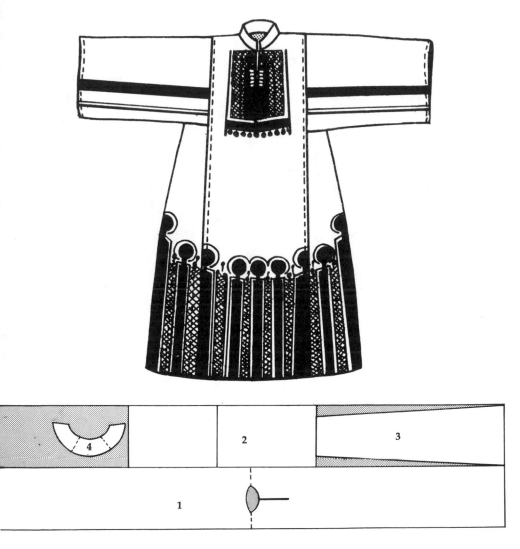

1 front and back   2 sleeves   3 side   4 collar

Designer/model: Marcia Reed, photographer: Richard Reed

This shirt was inspired by a tunic from Macedonia. The poppylike flower appliquéd on the front is in pale orange and is decorated with embroidery to complete the design. The black and red bands at the hemline and cuffs finish the edges. Using several prints allows a wide range of design possibilities, as seen in this example. Orange, blue, black, and red border prints are combined on the bodice, with a red butterfly print on the underarm panel. The sleeves and grosgrain-ribbon trim are bright red.

The bodice of this shirt is black, and the sleeves are two shades of orange. The reverse appliqué is black, red, and yellow. Yellow, green, and red grosgrain ribbons frame the inset. If you plan to use ribbon, it is advisable to preshrink it. The detail shows a playful bird. (For reverse-appliqué instructions see chapter 6.)

8. Holland

This fisherman's shirt from Holland was made of white cotton with narrow blue stripes. It had a narrow stand-up collar and a buttoned side closing. The 3/4-length sleeves were loose-fitting, as was the bodice. A small scarf was tied at the neck. Very full, baggy trousers that were banded at the knee, ribbed-wool stockings, and wooden shoes completed the costume.

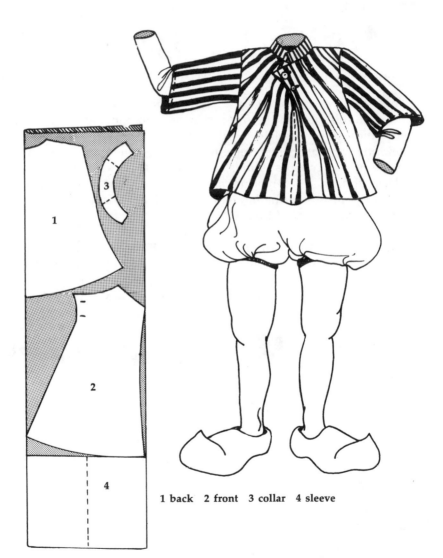

1 back 2 front 3 collar 4 sleeve

This casual shirt is made of white cotton gauze. It has a small collar and 3/4-length sleeves. A butterfly embroidered in chain stitches and french knots decorates the front. The design is stitched in shades of purple and turquoise.

Designer: Linda Edison, model: B. Johnson, photographer: Linda Edison

9. *Panama*

Molas are reverse appliqués made by the Indian women of the San Blas Islands in Panama. It is believed that the mola art form is directly related to the way in which these Indians painted their bodies years ago. Traders introduced fabrics, needles, threads, and scissors, and the painted designs were interpreted in cotton fabrics. The designs on the reverse-appliquéd squares are drawn from the artists' visual experiences. The style of the blouse is simple, with the appliquéd squares placed at the lower front and back. A yoke with a plain neckline and short, straight sleeves completed the garment.

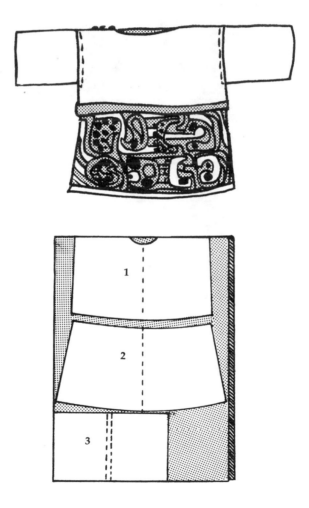

1 top front and back   2 bottom front and back   3 sleeves

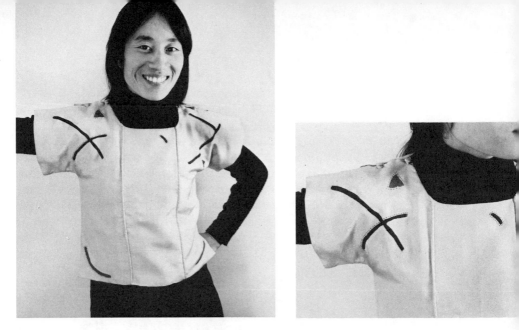

Designer/model: Becky Yamaguchi Kanow, photographer: C. Kanow

This mola-inspired design is made of canary-yellow silk with matching piping and is fully lined for added weight. A simple design is reverse-appliquéd in emerald green and pale blue, accenting the garment. Construction lines were changed to accommodate the fabric width.

An unusual mola design from the San Blas Indians was the starting point for this short top. The bodice is made of black cotton. It fastens on the shoulder and under the arm. The sleeves are very short, and corded bias bands finish the hems.

Designer/model: Colleen Miner, photographer: Skip Reedy

25

10. Italy

This ecclesiastical garment worn by Christian priests developed from Roman costumes. The shirtlike vestment was called a *dalmatica*. The finished style was attained in the Renaissance period and has remained the same ever since, except for slight variations of shape and decoration. The fabrics were dark velvets, decorated with gold and silk embroidery, brocade, or braid. Less elegant garments were made of linen with woven or embroidered bands.

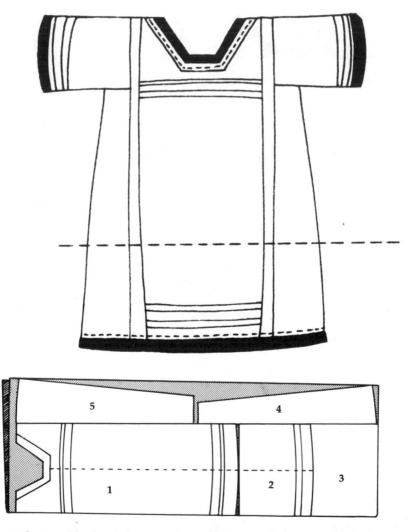

1 front and back   2 sleeve   3 sleeve facing   4 side front   5 side back

This shirt was inspired by a religious garment, which was very simply cut. Three different fabrics are blended: blue and white ikat was used for the back, side front, and lower part of the sleeves; front and back appliqués were done in primary colors; a Guatemalan striped material trimmed with ribbons and braid completes the shirt. Tiny metal buttons add the final touch to make this top an unusual one.

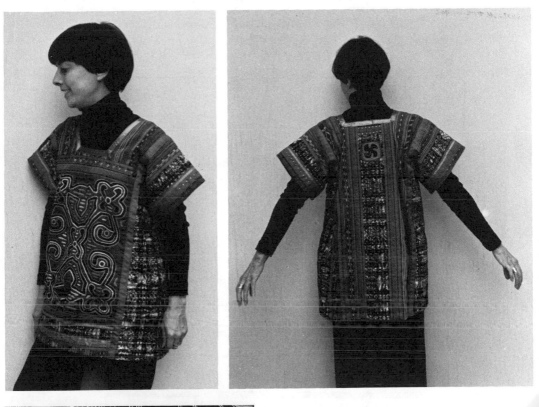

Designer/model: Annabel Woodsmall,
photographer: Roger Woodsmall

11. Indonesia

This jacket from Indonesia consists of tapa cloth, which is made by pounding paper mulberry bark until it is flat and thin. This beaten bark is cut into convenient pieces, and designs are painted on it with black, brown, or reddish-brown dyes. These jackets were worn with tapa sarongs, shell necklaces, and headdresses embellished with feathers and shells.

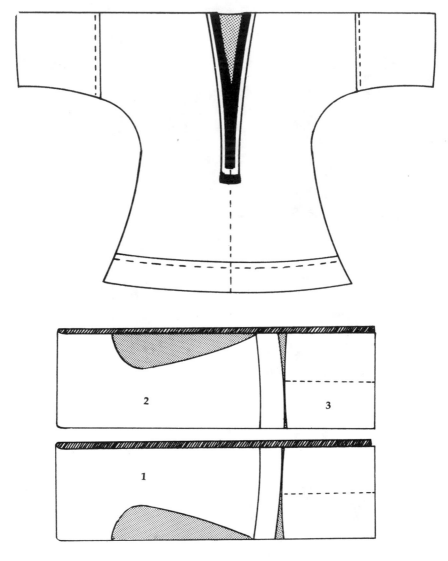

1 front   2 back   3 sleeves

This shirt exhibits an unusual combination of materials. The main body is made of rust and blue-gray handwoven wool twill. The appliquéd bands on the front and sleeves are Navajo velveteen, star-patterned acetate, handwoven Mexican cotton, and batiked fabric (originally a bedspread). The contrasting fur cuffs balance the weight of the shirt. The tunic fastens at the shoulders with handmade wooden buttons. The bands in front end in wool tassels (described in chapter 6). The sides of the shirt are faced and slit to allow for more freedom of movement.

Designer: Jo Diggs,
model: Valerie Currier,
photographer: Tom Retroff

29

12. Ancient Rome

Men and women in early Roman times wore very similar styles. The main garments were the shirt, or *tunica*, and the cloak worn over it, known as a toga. The *tunica* was actually an undergarment or indoor dress. It was considered improper to be seen outside the home without a toga. The shirt was cut fairly wide so that it could be pulled over the head and was knee-length. The fabrics used were wool and cotton. Various badges, usually in the form of narrow to wide purple stripes, indicated the wearer's rank or calling.

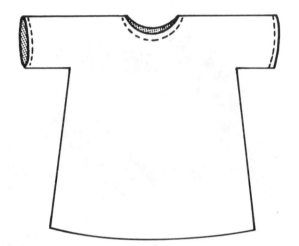

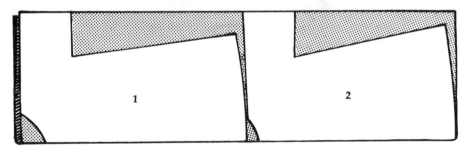

1 front   2 back

This embroidered oriental silk tapestry depicts children and an important man on a horse. His importance is evident from the fact that the rider is much larger than his mount. The red panel was stitched in shades of soft green, purple, and magenta silk floss. The tunic is made of silk in the same colors as the embroidery and lined in fine silk. It has knot buttons and loops made of rayon rattail, a silky cord.

Designer/model: Lois Ericson, photographer: Diane Ericson Frode

31

13. France

In medieval times shopkeepers and craftspeople wore very simple cotton or linen shirts over their pants or skirts. Some type of apron usually partially covered the plain, long shirt. Buttons were sometimes attached at the open slit at the neck to fasten the shirt, and tie belts were common.

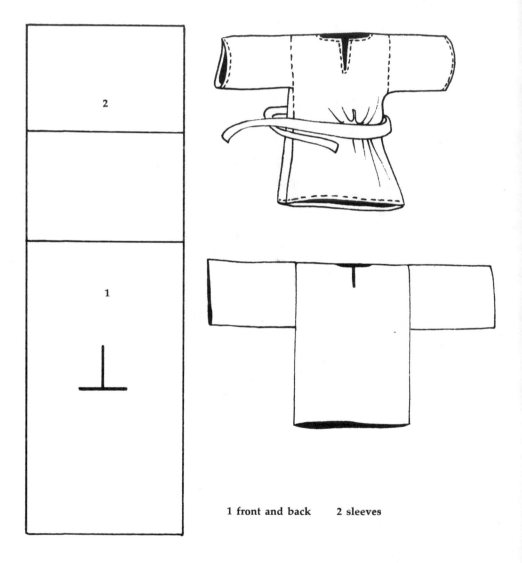

1 front and back   2 sleeves

Orange silk tweed and blue wool are combined in this supple hand-woven fabric. The style chosen for this shirt is very simple in order to minimize sewing and to use the 22″ (56cm) width of material effectively. The bodice is cut in one piece, with a slit for the neck opening, which was made as the fabric was woven. The woven pattern along the borders makes a nice finish.

Designer/model: Suzanne Ness O'Curry, photographer: Ron Wrona

14. Egypt

In Egypt the *eri* is a man's shirt, usually made of dark cotton or woolen fabric. It was a typical garment for the common people in the late 19th century, and it is probably still in use today. This shirt is worn with wide drawstring trousers, called *sserual*, and a cap with a blue silk tassel, called a *tarboush*.

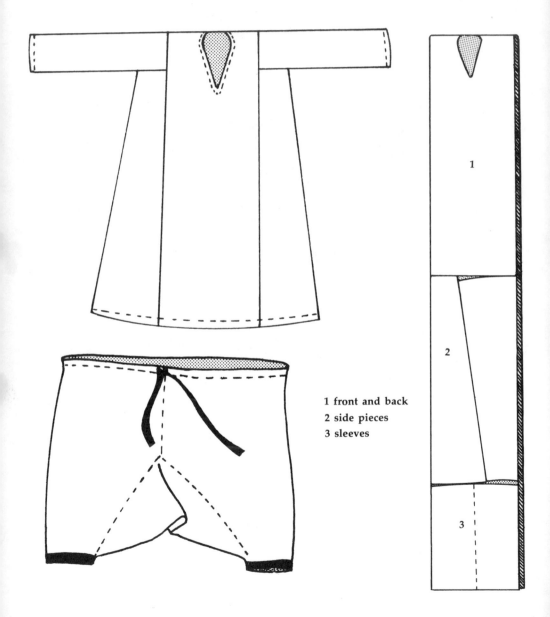

1 front and back
2 side pieces
3 sleeves

Patchwork strips in shades of purple, blue, rust, pale orange, dark green, and small accents of lime green are appliquéd to the front panel and cuffs of this shirt. The main body is made of heavy gráy-green cotton. The pieces are cut into strips and sewn together to make a design; the colors can be planned or chosen at random. The design is then sewn to the lining fabric. Complete instructions are given in chapter 6.

Designer: Lois Ericson, model: Mike Ericson, photographer: Diane Ericson Frode

15. Egypt

This 19th-century Egyptian women's garment is called a *sebleh* and is very similar to the African *tobe* and other loose-fitting garments from Arabia. The material for this tunic was usually indigo-dyed cotton. Ordinary *seblehs* are very plain, sometimes with a touch of coarse silk-floss embroidery at the neck opening. Wealthy women wear *seblehs* made of watered marked silk, taffeta, and black cotton with silk stripes.

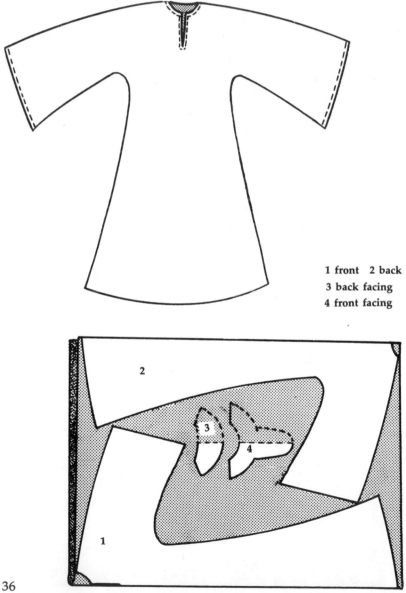

1 front   2 back
3 back facing
4 front facing

This batiked tunic gives the effect of "built-in" jewelry around the yoke, with the rest of the design fanning out from it. The colors are soft gray, charcoal, brown, rust, and orange. The fabric is a fine cotton, an excellent choice for the batik process. Silk, another natural fiber, is also suitable.

Designer/photographer:
Betty Auchard,
model: Renée Auchard

16. China

This wide-sleeved jerkin was worn by a Chinese woman of rank. Often enhanced with cloud and dragon patterns, these handwoven silk garments were lined in contrasting exotic fabrics and finished with ornate gold appliqué around the neck and front opening. Characteristic fasteners were knotted buttons and loops. The dragon motif represents the universe. When the garment is worn, the symbolism is complete. The ing details. Satin and chain stitches and french knots were used for the beautiful embroidery. Using appliquéd pieces underneath the embroidery shades the colors and creates more dimension.

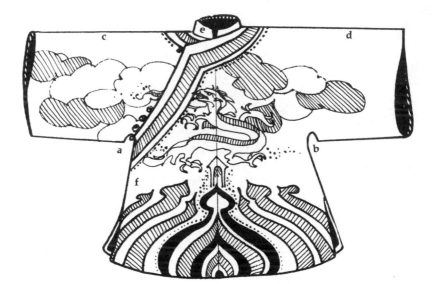

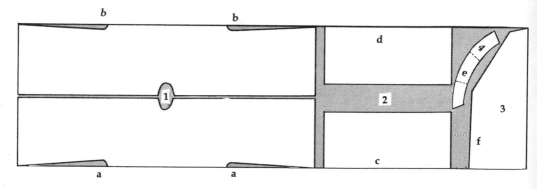

1 front and back   2 lower sleeve   3 front lapped section   4 collar

Designer/model: Lois Ericson,
photographer: Diane Ericson Frode

Designer/model: Diane Ericson Frode,
photographer: Chas Frode

The contemporary interpretation of this style is constructed of iridescent raw silk and fully lined with emerald green silk. The piece is enhanced with an original dragon design worked in appliqué and stitchery. Handmade piping and knotted buttons are handsome finishing details. Satin and chain and french knots were used for the beautiful embroidery. Using appliquéd pieces underneath the embroidery shades the colors and creates more dimension.

This Chinese silk tapestry is a reproduction of a painting by Emperor Hui Tsung dating from 1100 A.D. called *White Goose and Red Polygonum*, which was the inspiration for this oriental shirt. The fabric is beige polyester gabardine; the appliqués are silk and fine cotton. A filmy piece of silk organza covers most of the design to protect the tapestry and to soften the effect. The piping was made from bias bands cut from old silk dresses. The exquiste tapestry déserves special attention. Before being recycled it was the center of a pillow.

17. Italy

All ecclesiastical dress evolved from everyday garments, with particular styles adopted by various religious orders and used exclusively by the church. This surplice, which eventually became a choir robe, was worn over a fur robe in medieval times. Such surplices used lavish amounts of material, which was cut very full and gathered into a neckband. The sleeves were pieced and cut very full to resemble angel wings when the arms were raised.

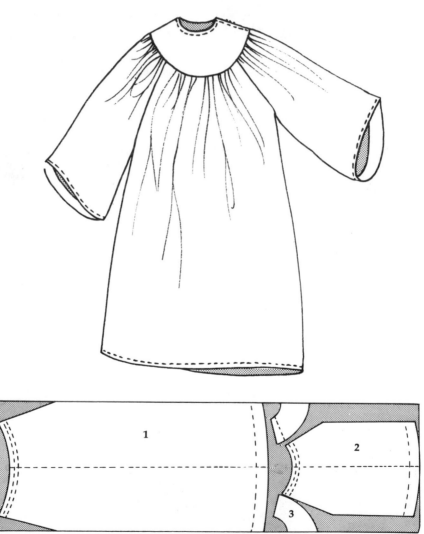

1 front and back   2 sleeves   3 yoke

Black plexiglass is appliquéd to this red satin tunic. Let your mind wander for a moment—this idea can spark many design possibilities. The plexiglass is pierced with a design to expose the satin and to accentuate the yoke and shape of the inset. The yoke extends over the shoulders, with the raglan sleeves, front, and back gathered at the yoke edge. The full sleeves are gathered at the wrist onto a straight cuff. The tunic is worn with black satin pants and ornately embroidered oriental boots.

Designer/model:
Perri Kimono,
photographer:
Jeorgia Anderson

41

18. Germany

The smock has been a very popular European garment since the 6th century. It is a loose-fitting shirt-type tunic that was worn by peasants of both sexes. The fabric was often linen or heavy cotton and was reversible. Embroidery was used not only to personalize the garment but also to denote the trade of the wearer.

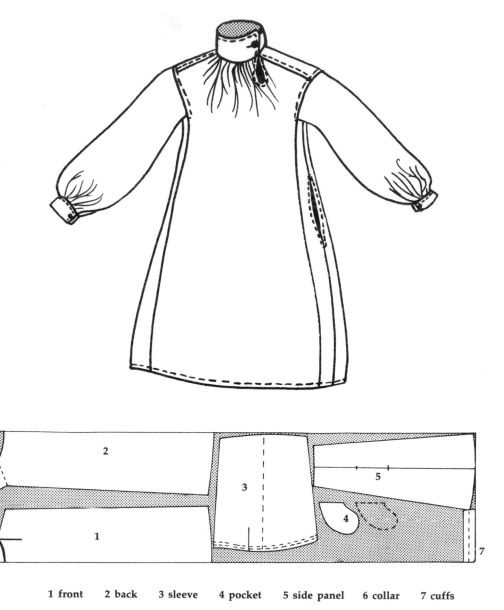

1 front   2 back   3 sleeve   4 pocket   5 side panel   6 collar   7 cuffs

This smock is constructed of handwoven Guatemalan fabric and embellished with shi-sha mirrors and perle-cotton embroidery. (Mirror embroidery is explained in chapter 6.) The creative stitchery includes cretan stitch, french knots, and flystitch and is used abundantly on the sleeves and collar. Stitching solid areas over the striped fabric gives it an entirely different effect—one is not aware of the stripes on the sleeve insets and the collar. The colors of the stripes are red, yellow, charcoal, and light green.

Designer/photographer: Joanne Purpus, model: Leslie Suzuki

CHAPTER II.

The Dress

In the early 1800s even refined women damped their summer dresses to reveal voluptuous figures.

1. India

This man's cotton tunic originated in India in the region known as Kashmir, which is famous for the fine goat wool called cashmere. The cut of this shirt is very geometric, with square armholes, straight front and back panels, and flared side panels. For ease of movement small triangular gussets were inserted under the arm. The typical fabric for this shirt was tie-dyed cotton, with silk embroidery, mirrors, and bits of red cloth appliquéd on the front panel. The neck opening fastened with small buttons and loops.

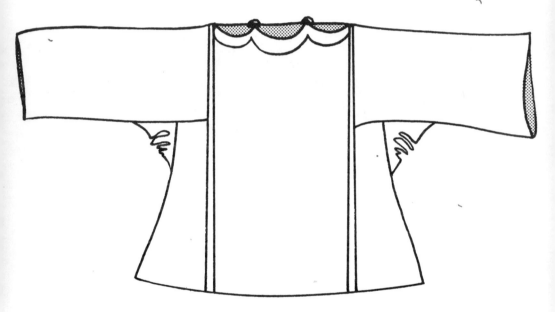

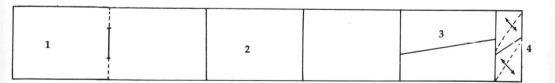

1 front and back   2 sleeves   3 side pieces   4 gussets

Gold and purple silk pongee and crepe were chosen for this beautiful tunic, worn with a long skirt. The designs were hand-painted, block-printed, and batiked. French seams, reversed so that small ridges are evident on the side and back seams, make a nice finish. Handmade glass beads were used for the closures.

Designer: Anna Polesny, model: Beverly Rohe, photographer: Greg Mayhood

2. *Alaska*

The Northwest Coast Indians of Alaska made shirts from navy and black Hudson Bay blankets, which were acquired from traders in the 18th and 19th centuries. Red flannel accents were appliquéd onto the blanket material. Fish and bird designs were common; they were created by sewing hundreds of shell disks to the shirt. Pearl buttons were later used instead of the shells.

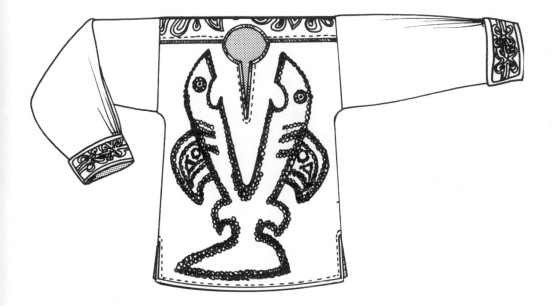

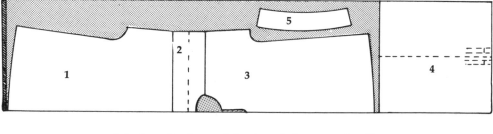

1 back   2 yoke   3 front   4 sleeves   5 cuffs

The body of this dress is navy blue, with two bright red appliquéd and stenciled birds (chapter 6). Shades of rust, light blue, lavender, and finished with a bias band and beading. (Stenciling, patchwork, and bias trim are described in chapter 6.) The hem is appliquéd to emphasize with french knots. The sleeves are machine-quilted. The neck edge is finished with a bias band and beading. Stenciling, patchwork, and bias trim are described in Chapter 6.) The hem is appliquéd to emphasize the side slits.

Designer/model: Diane Ericson Frode, photographer: Chas Frode

3. Palestine

This beautiful ankle-length dress from Palestine has long sleeves that are slightly narrowed at the wrist. There are three side panels to make it flare gracefully. The front and back yokes are perfect places to add decoration. The original dress was made of coarse cotton with abundant silk embroidery. Taffeta in bright colors was sometimes inserted to further enrich these garments.

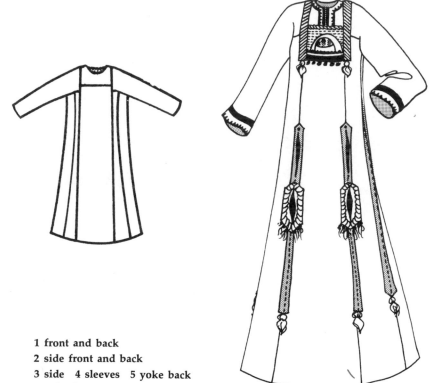

1 front and back
2 side front and back
3 side   4 sleeves   5 yoke back
6 yoke front   7 pockets

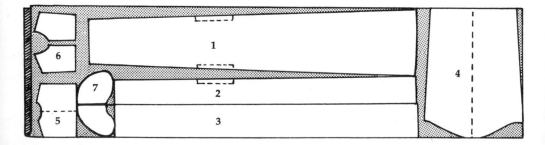

The simple style of this garment makes a perfect background for intricate embellishment. The beautiful fabric is handwoven wool, using a fine white weft and a subtly striped warp. The original designs have been interpreted in woven trims rather than in embroidery. The card-woven bands, with slits for the pocket, are sewn to the garment, as are the other small bands that trim the lower section of the dress. All the bands are handsomely done in primary colors. The two small bands at the neck consist of Bolivian double-faced weave, using the design of the mola inset as part of the front yoke. The trims, including the mola, are South American in design and color combination, so this garment is truly an ethnic mixture.

Designer/model: Enola Dickey,
photographer: Brack Brown

51

4. India

This child's dress from India was made of cotton mirrored cloth with lavish amounts of hand embroidery. The high-waisted bodice is fitted with a gathered skirt and a border design. The long sleeves have embroidered bands at the cuff.

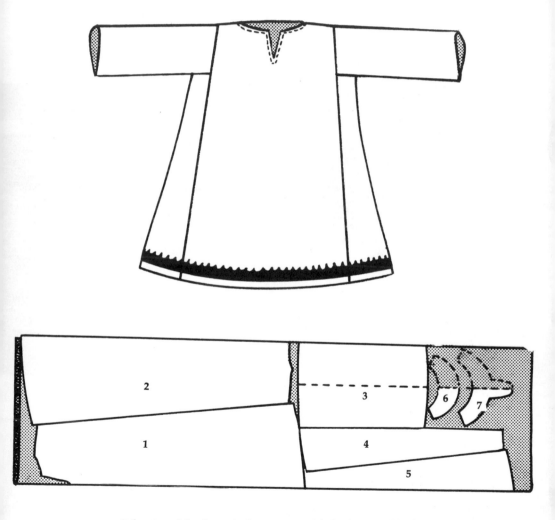

1 front   2 back   3 sleeves   4 side back   5 side front

6 facing back   7 facing front

An Indian child's dress, obtained at a secondhand sale, was the inspiration for this long tunic. The sleeves of the original dress consisted of mirror cloth banded by braid, with the traditional elephant design woven in silver thread. The garment was taken apart, retaining the sleeves and bands, which became the front and back panels. The fabric used for the body of the dress is coarse red handwoven cotton. The front panel is black, with grosgrain ribbon and braid in shades that repeat the colors of the mirror cloth. A woven sash is sewn in the side seams, and the sleeves are banded to give the appearance of a ruffle at the cuff. The "ruffle" is faced with black to correspond with the front and back panels.

Designer/model: Salley Voss, photographer: Annabel Woodsmall

53

5. Turkestan

This woman's shirt from Turkestan was made of very soft, lightweight silk. The background color was rose, with white and yellow flowers. The hems, collar, and front closure were piped in black. This tunic was worn with sheepskin riding breeches that were appliquéd with yellow silk and embroidered with green, purple, and red silk floss. A red velvet jacket with silver stitching completed this colorful costume.

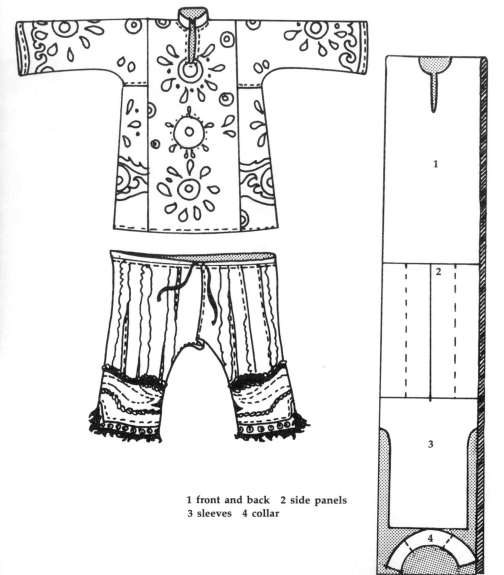

1 front and back   2 side panels
3 sleeves   4 collar

Designer/model: Marcia Reed,
photographer: Richard Reed

Designer/model: Diane Ericson Frode,
photographer: Chas Frode

The needlepoint insets on the sleeves and yoke give the color scheme of this dress. Purple, red, yellow, blue, green, and off-white are combined effectively. When the material is pieced, the shapes are overlapped and topstitched. The raw seams are covered with grosgrain ribbon, which makes finishing easy. This process also accentuates the colored shapes on the dress. The green and yellow tassel accents the front panel. (Tassels are described in chapter 6.)

The duck on the front of this dress is woven in shades of yellow and off-white. The technique is a simple one: slash the fabric in 1/4" strips to make the warp; weave into the warp with yarn or rag strips; line the back of the design. (See chapter 6 for weaving techniques.) The sleeves are made of beige and tan cotton and off-white linen. Natural linen ravels easily, and it was left unfinished to accentuate this feature. French knots accent the front panels. The main body of the dress is made of two shades of tan Calcutta cloth.

6. Babylon

This long, simple tunic from Babylon is cut from a single pattern piece. The shoulder seams are sewn partway, with buttons and loops to fasten the neck. The sides are open to the knee to allow ease of movement. The designs near the hem of this elegant tunic represent the tree of life, a symbol that has been used for centuries. The geometric embroidery was done in a needle-weaving technique similar to the method used by the ancient Egyptians.

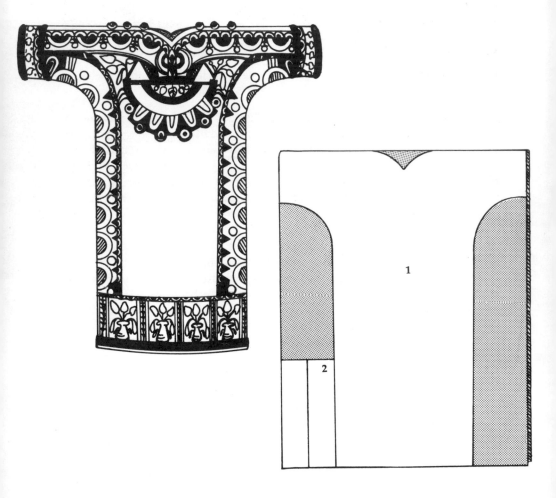

1 front and back   2 sleeve bands

This jumper dress is made of English wool in a blue-gray herringbone weave. The yoke is embroidered with Persian wools and incorporates mother-of-pearl disks and buttons. The garment is lined, and it fastens at both shoulders with self-covered buttons.

Designer/photographer: Joanne Purpus, model: Leslie Suzuki

7. England

The English smock was a very popular garment in the 18th and 19th centuries, although it was not worn by women and children until the late 1800s. It was worn by farmers and tradespeople to protect their clothes. Some smocks were special and were used only for formal occasions; these were usually handed down in the family. This reversible tunic was made of linen or cotton twill. All the pieces in the garment are rectangular. The center front, back, and upper sleeves were gathered in a wide band, which was embroidered to retain the fullness. The stitching looks very complicated, but often only three stitches were used—chain, feather, and outline. (These stitches are discussed in chapter 6.)

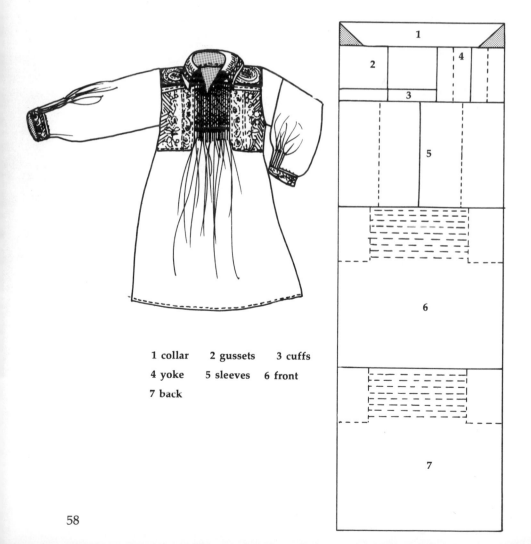

1 collar   2 gussets   3 cuffs

4 yoke   5 sleeves   6 front

7 back

This adaptation of the English smock is made of twill-woven navy denim, which is similar in weight to the original fabric. It is lavishly embroidered with a pale gray-green embroidery floss. The buttons are made of pewter, which complements the stitching. If the smock buttoned all the way down the front, it could be used as a coat.

Designer/model: Diane Ritch,
photographer: Beebo Turman

8. Africa

The *tobe* is a garment from Africa. It was made of 3"-wide strips of woven cotton that were sewn together. The flared effect was created by gussets inserted between the strips. This *tobe* was white with subtle cream stripes. The handsome design was embroidered on the chest in ivory-colored thread. The lower part of the design was embroidered on the large pocket.

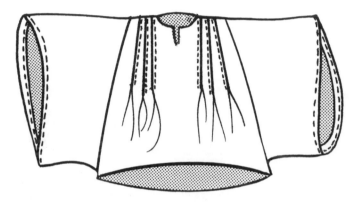

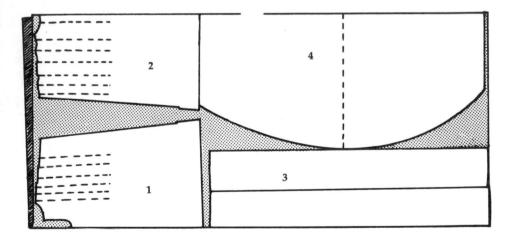

1 front   2 back   3 sleeve facing   4 sleeves

The original *tobe* shirt was lengthened into a dress. Wine cotton velveteen is the fabric used in the main body. Tiny beads are sewn at the neck edge. Silk piping accentuates the pleats over the shoulders. The wide sleeves and bands at the bottom are indigo and magenta block-printed birds.

Designer: Anna Polesny, model: Beverly Rohe, photographer: Greg Mayhood

9. Ancient Egypt

The Copts were the first Christian converts in ancient Egypt. They wore simple, loose-fitting garments. In 300 A.D. decoration was first added to what had been very plain tunics. These decorative motifs were treasured and were often removed from an old garment and sewn to a new one. The fabric used for these tunics was natural linen. The decorative bands were made of wool and linen, which were dyed in various shades of red, blue, yellow, green, and orange. The simple style of this Coptic garment persisted for many centuries.

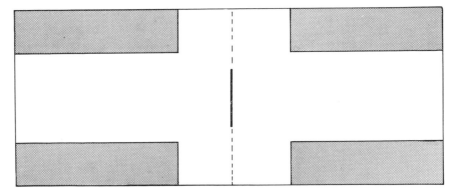

The cut of this simple dress, made from just one pattern piece, provides uninterrupted space for decoration. It is painted with dye and heat-set by the sun or with an iron. (See the list of suppliers at the back of the book.) The dye can be brushed on, block-printed, or stenciled. The colors chosen for this tunic are purple, red, and yellow-orange on an off-white cotton fabric.

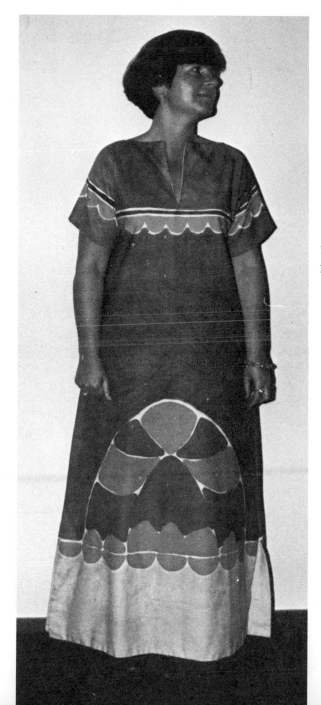

Designer/model: Berta Bray,
photographer: Patricia Bolfing

10. Ancient Egypt

The *kalasiris* is a simply shaped linen garment that dates from 1400 B.C. Egypt. It was worn by people of all social classes, with relative wealth determining the materials and embellishments used. One piece of material was folded in the middle and sewn on the sides, leaving openings for the armholes. The *kalasiris* was belted, and the neckline was either round or slit. The fabric was sometimes printed with small geometric designs.

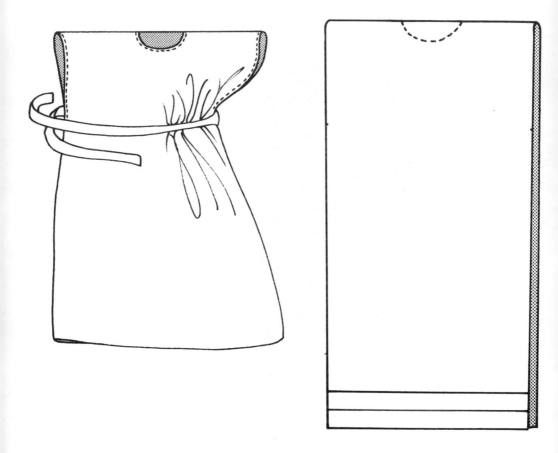

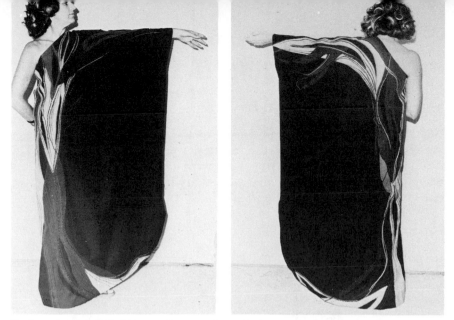

Designer/model: B.J. Adams, photographer: Clark Adams

This dress was inspired by both the *kalasiris* and an Indian sari. It is made of black gabardine, with cotton and linen appliqués in shades of brown, beige, and mat gold. The tree appliqué and embroidery consist of both machine- and handwork. Perle cotton is couched by hand to emphasize the lines in the tree. The trunk goes up one side of the dress, the branches over one shoulder, and the roots along the hem.

Flowers and leaves were generously appliquéd and embroidered on a fine cotton-batiste tablecloth, which was recycled and itself appliquéd to a long dress made of blue-green acrylic. The sleeves were cut in a round shape so that the border of the round cloth could form the edge.

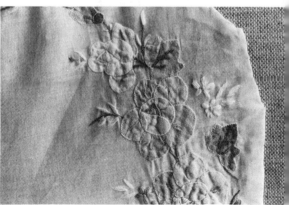

Designer/model: Lois Ericson,
photographer: Diane Ericson Frode

11. Ancient Egypt

This is another style of *kalasiris*, which is cut very narrow. To give elasticity and freedom of movement to the wearer, the garment was knitted very loosely so that the material was almost transparent. The tunic was ankle-length and was worn with a belt. An intricate necklace resembling a large circular collar was a very important accessory for the rich.

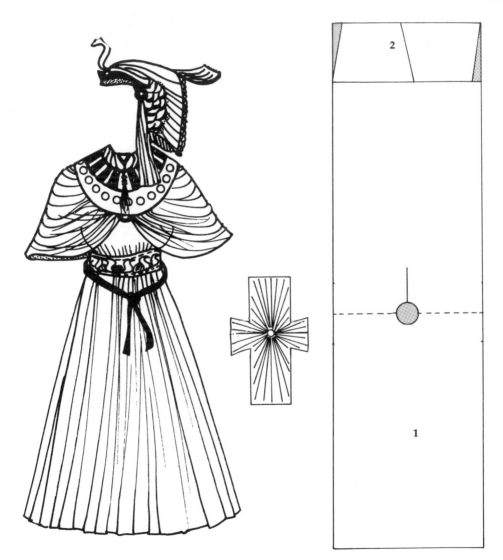

1 front and back   2 sleeves

This tunic is called "the Pharaoh" by the designer, who was inspired by ancient Egyptian art and costume. It is made of polyester-cotton poplin in a khaki color to represent desert sand. The front of the tunic features a machine-quilted illustration based on the carvings on Amenhotep's tomb. It was achieved by drawing the design on tracing paper, overlaying the paper on two layers of poplin separated by polyester batting, and stitching through the paper with blue thread. The paper was then torn away, the batting trimmed, and the entire motif machine-appliquéd to the front of the tunic. The repeat pattern around the neckline was also machine-stitched. Hieroglyphic designs were stenciled on the sleeves and bottom of the tunic, using blue acrylic textile paint. (See chapter 6 for stenciling instructions.)

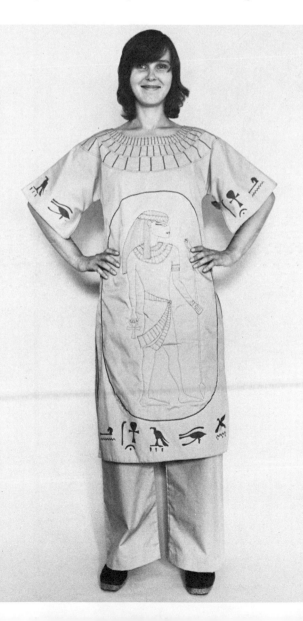

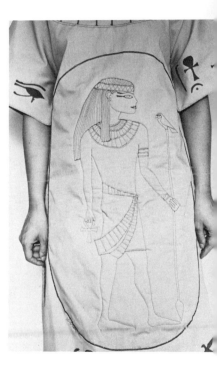

Designer: Susan Grant,
model: Florence Tracz

12. Syria

This Syrian dress was originally made of silk and cotton, with hand-embroidered panels that are beautifully executed in satin and chain stitches. The dress is dark blue with red and green stripes. The panel, embroidered in green, red, blue, and yellow, is a large square that forms a triangle effect on the front and back. Gussets under the arms allow freedom of movement, and the side panels give a nice flare to the skirt. The yoke effect suggests a loose collar on top of a plain dress.

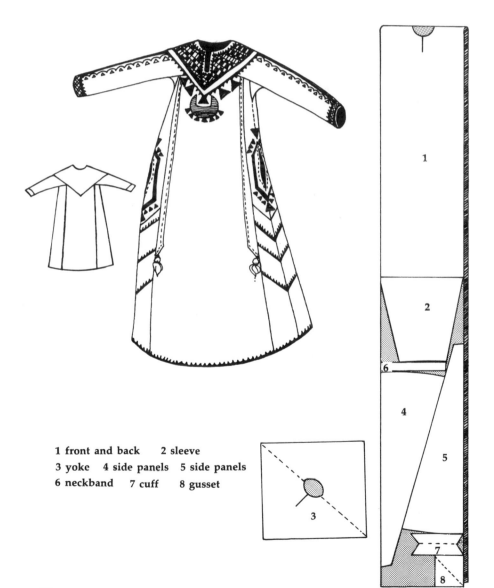

1 front and back   2 sleeve
3 yoke   4 side panels   5 side panels
6 neckband   7 cuff   8 gusset

This garment is completely handwoven to conform to the wearer's contours and to flow gracefully from the triangular yoke. The yoke and the card-woven trims are richly patterned and have interesting surface texture. The pocket slits, woven in the braid, are applied to the outside of the garment. The trim at the neck edge is shaped after weaving to conform to the curved edge. The yarns are blue, purple, and red-orange-rust wools.

Designer/model: Enola Dickey, photographer: Brack Brown

13. Afghanistan

This women's undergarment from Afghanistan is very colorful. The bodice is a small flowered cotton print in shades of yellow and red. The slit neck is bound with plain red and trimmed with small tin disks. The shirt and sleeves are made of dark blue cotton decorated with red, white, and yellow wax-paint designs. The white surfaces were then covered with a shiny powder, which adhered to the wax, creating an unusual effect. During the 16th century soldiers started to wear torn jackets, exposing their shirts through the slits. This style became especially popular in court dress. The slashed outer garments and the undergarments were usually made of contrasting fabrics.

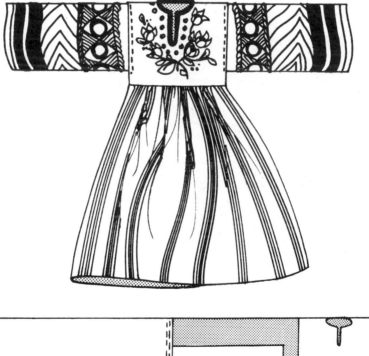

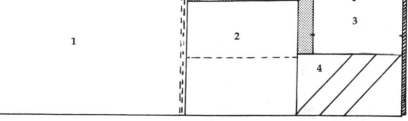

1 skirt front and back   2 sleeves   3 yoke front and back   4 neckbands

The inspiration for the decorative part of this dress was the slashing concept. The cut is basically that of the original undergarment but without the gathers. The long tunic is made of rust and gold washable wool. The slits on the sleeves and sides are hemmed. Another way to finish these slashes would be to line the garment with a contrasting material. The additional piece of fabric behind the slit is left loose for ease of movement. The dark-light embroidery highlights the interesting insets, hemmed edges, and yoke. The yoke and sleeves are cut in one piece.

Designer/model: Colleen Minor, photographer: Skip Reedy

14. *Saudi Arabia*

This design for a Bedouin desert robe comes from Saudi Arabia. This garment is still used by tribal chiefs in various ceremonies. It can be made of silk, brocade, or wool. The robe consists of one length of material, which is folded, hemmed at the neck opening, left open at the armhole, and sewn at the sides below the opening, in keeping with the traditional simplified lifestyle of this nomadic desert tribe.

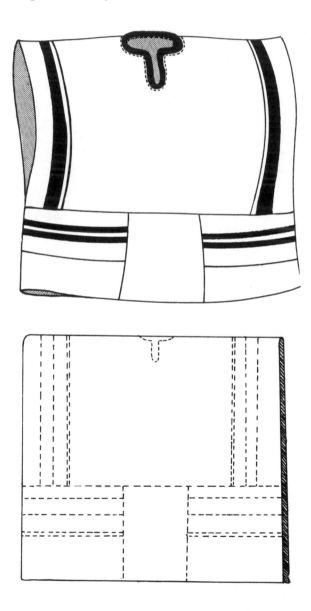

Block-printing and batik techniques are handsomely combined in this
garment. The ancient blocks used for the printing came from Iran. The
fabric used for this pieced robe is silk-and-cotton challis; the colors are
leather pants and decorated with wonderful painted designs. The tree
chapter 6 for instructions.)

Designer: Anna Polesny, model: Beverly Rohe, photographer: Greg Mayhood

15. Siberia

A Siberian shaman's costume consisted of a long leather tunic worn with leather pants, decorated with wonderful painted designs. The tree showed the route taken by the medicine man to the underworld in order to learn how to find good hunting places. The animals represent the game that he hoped to locate for the hunters of the tribe.

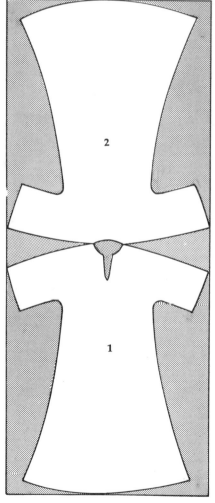

1 front   2 back

This hostess gown features a trapunto dragon motif. The gown is constructed of white nubbed polyester-cotton, with the design, collar, cuffs, and yoke cut from blue-and-white Dutch wax-resist cotton. The garment has wide sleeves, a small stand-up collar, and side slits to the knee. The dragon was drawn and then machine-stitched on a "sandwich" made of tissue paper, netting, and the Dutch fabric. When the paper was torn away, the netting was slit in specific places, which were stuffed with polyester fiberfill and resewn. The entire dragon was then machine-appliquéd to the front of the gown.

Designer: Susan Grant,
model: Florence Tracz

16. Burma

This short jacket from Burma, called an *eng Kji*, was made of a white cotton similar to glazed chintz, which was heavily padded and quilted. The quilting was done in a diagonal pattern on the main part of the garment and in narrow, straight lines on the cuffs, front closure, and bottom edge. The flap buttons underneath as well as on the asymmetrical front closing.

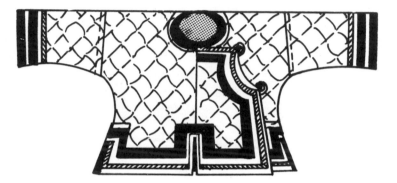

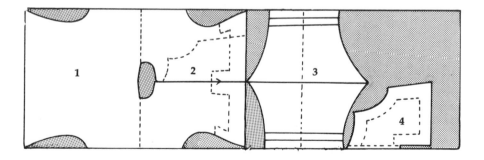

1 back   2 front   3 sleeves   4 front lap

Pale orange polyester gabardine was the fabric chosen for this evening dress, which could also be worn as a coat. The loose fit, wide sleeves, and wrapped look with loops and buttons give it an oriental feeling. The appliqués are made of linen napkins embroidered with very tiny cross-stitches and other sheer fabrics. The garment is fully lined with flowered voile, an unexpected feature.

Designer/model: Lois Ericson, photographer: Diane Ericson Frode

17. Egypt

An Egyptian caftan worn by women of rank is called a *yelek*. It buttoned at the waist and had slits up the sides. Fabrics ranged from cottons to silks and brocades. This coatlike garment was worn over a long crepe tunic and silk pants. A square of fabric folded in a triangle was tied around the hips, and an *aba*—a loose, sleeveless outergarment—was worn over the *yelek*.

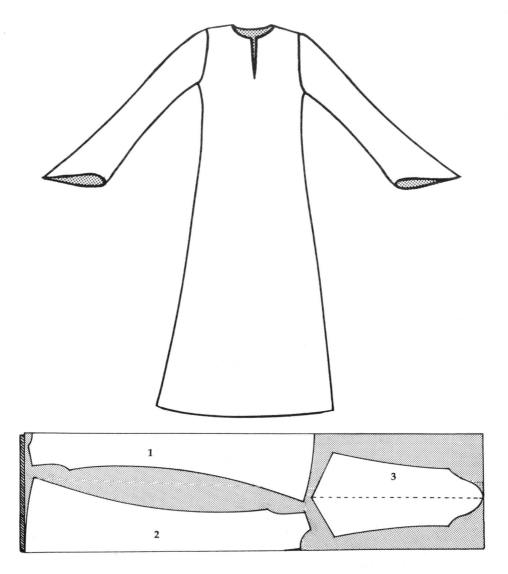

1 back   2 front   3 sleeves

Designer/photographer: Heidi Hybl, model: Suzi Lofaso

This caftan is made of dusty-rose no-wale corduroy. The philodendron leaves are made of machine-appliquéd green velour. The flowered bands are strips of cotton fabric. Embroidered tape could also be used to frame or accentuate a design in this way.

This long dress is made of an off-white linenlike fabric, with soft green and gold woven appliqués. These shaped tapestry pieces were fastened to the garment and extended with stitchery onto the bodice and down the sleeves. The tapestry sections were inspired by the designs made by ocean tides on sand. The dress is worn with a wrapped necklace made of glass, metal, and amber beads.

Designer/model: Lois Ericson,
photographer: Diane Ericson Frode

79

18. American Indian

A two-skins dress was worn by some of the Plains Indian tribes. The front and back were cut in the same shape, each from one skin. A yoke extending from one wrist to the other with an opening for the neck was added. It was usually heavily beaded or decorated with quillwork. Porcupine and various bird quills were dyed, sorted according to size, and flattened before sewing in place.

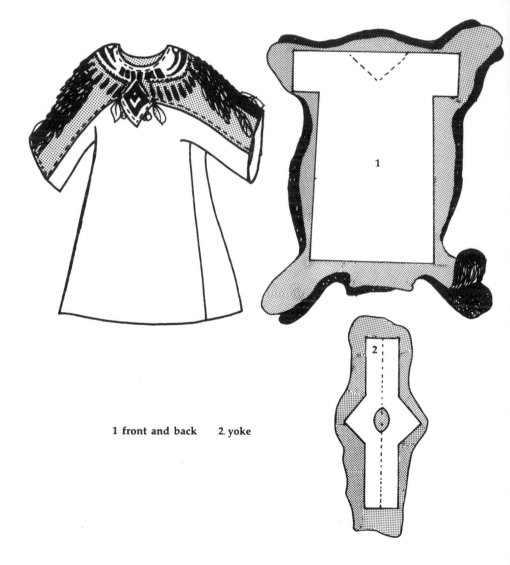

1 front and back   2. yoke

The use of black can lend a dramatic effect to a clothing design. This example features appliqué in primary colors on the front. Rows of couching border the appliqué, ending in the leaf shapes at the bottom, and encircle the stand-up collar. The leaf shapes are repeated on the shoulder in a cutwork technique. (Cutwork is described in chapter 6.) Tiny beads are sewn on the bodice and sleeves and worked into the fringe at the sleeve edges.

Designer/model: Marcia Reed, photographer: Richard Reed

19. Russia

A *kiba* is a Finnish garment from a settlement near the Volga River in Russia. It was made of coarse natural linen with red bands intermixed with glass beads covering the side front seams. The bands at the neck opening, sleeve, and hem consisted of diagonal ribbon stitching and embroidery, with plain red strips on either side. Over this belted shirt women wore an ornamental apron made of leather and red wool and decorated with coins and beads. Underneath they wore long linen drawers and horizontally pleated boots. Their heads were covered with a silk scarf, topped by a fancy hat.

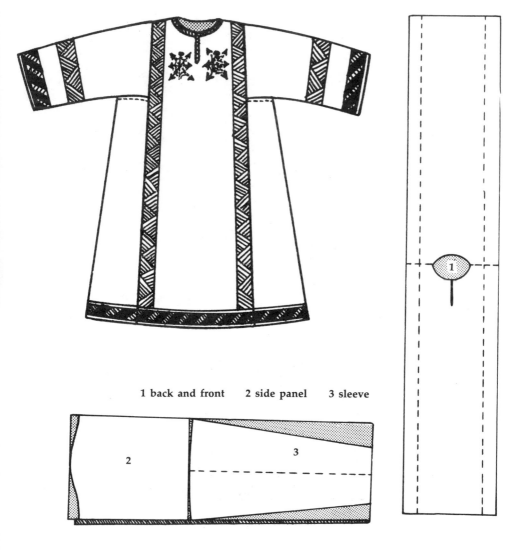

1 back and front   2 side panel   3 sleeve

Designer/model: Jean Hudson,
photographer: Ray Highfill

This Easter dress was aptly named "Joy" by the designer. It is made of pink rayon that looks like raw silk. The maroon letter designs are machine-appliquéd.

The long dress at the left is made of cotton with old lace and appliqué. The seams are embroidered, and tiny beads are sewn over the shoulders. The long slits on the front seams are bound with a rust, dark green, purple, cream, and gold print fabric. The short version of this dress at right features a handworked flower design done in textile paint on a synthetic fabric. The rest of the dress is made of coordinating black and yellow cottons. The smaller flower designs are hand-embroidered. The sleeve and neck facings are reversed to the right side, and the raw edges are covered with ribbon. Both garments are completely washable.

Designer: Berta Bray,
models: Lynn Dempsey
and Judy Dempsey,
photographer: Patricia Bolfing

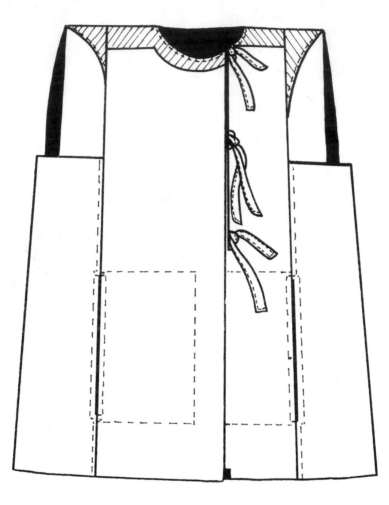

CHAPTER III.

The Vest

In 1665 the vest was introduced as a part of a man's wardrobe. This sleeveless tunic was derived from a doublet, and it linked the garments of the past with those of the present.

1. England

Knights in the 13th century wore chain mail with a padded underjacket of coarse cotton. Chain mail was made by joining links together: about 250,000 links and 3 years were required to make one suit. In the early 1300s craftsmen began to shape plates and to join them together to the vest is lined separately and faggoted together for an interesting effect. (Faggoting is described in chapter 6.) The design on the front and pocket is made from the directions for making the toy plus some

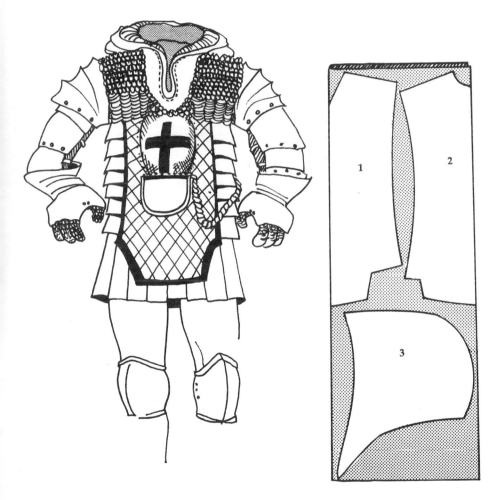

1 front   2 back   3 hood

patchwork. The rabbit is appliquéd to a natural cotton fabric and quilted to a sand-colored lining. This process makes the vest reversible, for the stitiching lines form the design when the lining side is out. The facings serve as a decorative element when turned to the outside of the garment and are accented with peach satin piping. (See chapter 6 for facings.)

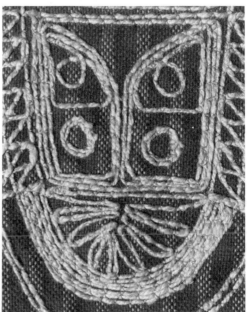

Designer/model: Annabel Woodsmall,
photographer: Roger Woodsmall

2. China

In China there is a tradition of uniformity in dress, which results from the belief that all people have a common beginning in the distant past. The materials and color combinations used offer opportunities for variety. Silk, cotton, and even straw are used in some of the warmer areas. The silks and cottons are quilted and fur-lined to give warmth in the colder regions. This 19th-century boy's vest was quilted for winter wear. It was made of red silk, a color which denotes happiness, prosperity, and good fortune.

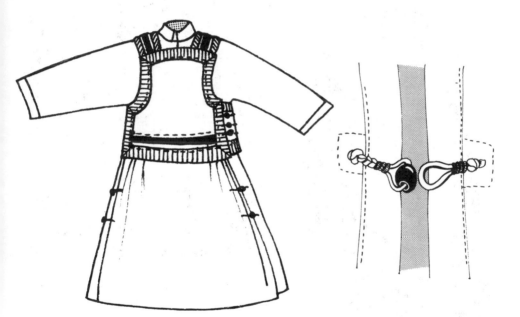

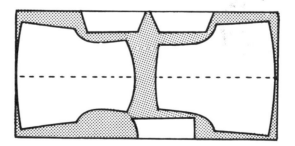

The main body of this vest is made of red and green felt, with balancing blue stripes. The felt pieces are joined together with ribbons in bold colors. The binding around the edges and straps of the vest is made of Japanese *kasuri* cotton and purple velvet, with yellow bias cording. The closings on each side are made of rattail braid loops and red glass buttons.

Designer/photographer:
Pamela Magnuson,
model: Sue Venturino

3. Burma

A very simple vest from Burma was made of blue velvet and edged with red cotton bias bands. The waistcoat fastened with buttons and loops. A cotton jacket, embroidered with silk, was usually worn over the vest. A very bright woven and embroidered skirt and shoulder bag completed the costume.

1 front   2 back

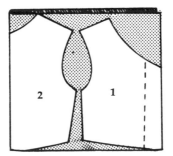

Designer: Nancy Love, photographer: Hannah Tandeta

This short vest utilizes some very unusual fabrics from Japan. The lively prints are appliquéd onto red denim. The design of the machine quilting emphasizes the circular lines of the flower on the front and back. Silver buttons and loops form the asymmetrical closing. All the seams are covered with silk ribbon or bias banding.

The rabbit on this vest is a reproduction of an antique stuffed toy. The pocket is made of the directions for making the toy plus some patchwork. The rabbit is appliquéd to a natural cotton fabric and quilted to a sand-colored lining. This process makes the vest reversible, for the stitching lines form the design when the lining side is out. The facings serve as a decorative element when turned to the outside of the garment and are accented with peach satin piping. (See chapter 6 for facings.)

Designer/model: Diane Ericson Frode,
photographer: Chas Frode

4. Russia

A short vest, made of red woolen damask, is part of the Great Russian costume. The curved bands on the design are made of appliquéd silver braid. The armholes and neck edges are finished with black velvet. At the lower hem a thick roll of coarse linen is sewn. The vest fastens at the center front with hook and eyes.

A sun design was chosen to decorate this black knit vest. The top half of the design is made of appliquéd gold knit fabric with some stitchery. The lower half, the rays, is embroidered with gold, orange, and red chain stitches. The edges of this sleeveless jacket are bound in red.

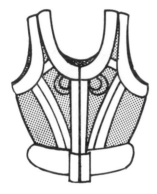

1 front   2 back   3 front hem bands
4 back neck facing   5 front neck facing
6 armhole facing

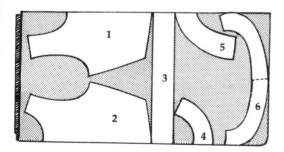

**Designer/model: Linda Edison,
photographer: B. Johnson**

5. Europe

In many European countries during the Middle Ages a tabard was worn over a suit of armor. The function of the tabard was to eliminate the glare of the sun on the armor. These garments were embroidered with the arms of the wearer—hence the phrase "coat of arms." When this style of tunic was adopted by ordinary citizens, it was worn over a *bliaud* (shirt). The tabard was rectangular in shape, with a round, square, or slit neck opening. It fastened with ties, buttons, or buckles on the sides. It was usually made of a heavy fabric such as wool, with embroidered bands finishing the edges.

The tabard is a very comfortable garment, easily worn with pants, shirts, or dresses. This one is made of rust-colored cotton suedecloth. The soft brown crocheted pieces are sewn in place on top of the pocket sections. A gray ribbon is threaded through the open rows of the crochet. The vestlike garment is lined and tied on each side.

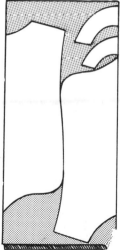

1 back   2 front
3 back facing
4 front facing

Designer/photographer: Diane Ericson Frode, model: Lois Ericson

Designer/photographer: Jo Diggs, model: Britt Anderson

The many shades of rose in this tunic project a subtle statement. The main body of this contemporary tabard is made of cotton denim. The front panel is of synthetic suede edged with cotton chintz. The quilted and appliquéd yoke is cotton and acetate with silk embroidery. The looped fringe across the front and on the sides is handspun wool. It appears to frame the "picture." The short tunic slips over the head and ties at the waist. It can be worn with long or short pants or dresses.

A warp-faced fabric in rose, wine, and blue was chosen for this tabard. The wine color is repeated on the front panel and combined with mirrors and embroidery. (Instructions for applying mirrors are given in chapter 6.) Grosgrain ribbons tie on the sides.

A design of wild grass blowing in the wind is stenciled on a white background on the front of this tabard. The fabric is a wash-and-wear gray cotton. The pocket is lined and stitched in place. This tabard fastens on the side with fabric loops and buttons.

Designer/model: Kristine Barrett,
photographer: Lois Ericson

Designer/model: Diane Ericson Frode,
photographer: Chas Frode

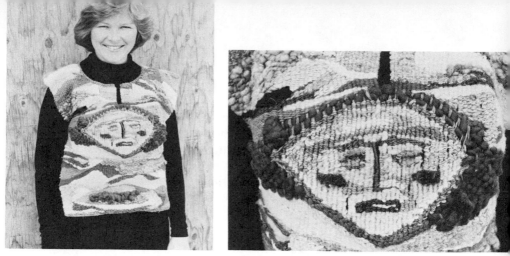

Designer: Dorie Riley, model: Diane Ericson Frode, photographer: Chas Frode

A tabard in warm colors is woven on a piece of cardboard. The warp is cotton carpet warp; the weft is wool, rayon, and synthetic yarn. This garment ties under the arms with crocheted chains. It was made as a beginning weaving project.

This warm sleeveless garment is made of heavy mustard-colored rib-woven melton wool. The hood and yokes are woven in the pin-weaving technique. Unspun fleece, yarn, and fabric cut into strips are woven in shades of gold and brown and accented with wrapping. The hood is lined with a dark brown knit. For added warmth detachable sleeves may be tied on if desired.

This vest is woven in shades of gray wool, with a rust stripe on the bottom border. The simple style is made from one piece of material, which is folded at the shoulders and sewn at the sides. The neckline is a slit, which was planned and made while the piece was being woven. It could be faced or fully lined if commercial fabric is used.

Designer/model: Diane Ericson Frode, photographer: Chas Frode

Designer/model: Suzanne Ness O'Curry, photographer: Ron Wrona

6. England

In Elizabethan times court dress was very elegant, with hooped dresses, starched collars or ruffs, and long veils. Men wore long colored hose, padded breeches, embroidered shirts, and doublets with removable sleeves. The same styles, greatly simplified, were worn by the peasants and storekeepers. More pratical materials were used: linen shirts, leather doublets, padded breeches, and black hose.

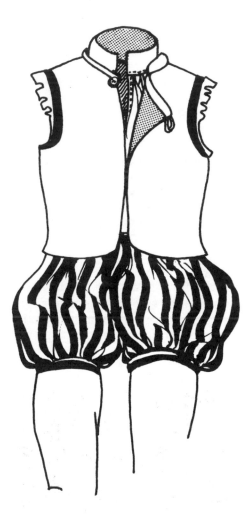

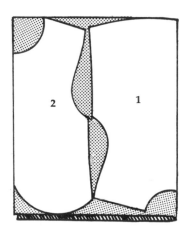

1 front   2 back

Designer/model: Colleen Minor, photographer: Skip Reedy

Since the 1920s the Seminole Indians of Florida have been sewing and wearing elaborate patchwork costumes. Skirts, blouses, and shirts are made of alternating solid and patchwork strips. The patchwork is made by cutting strips, sewing them together, cutting them either perpendicularly or at an angle, rearranging them, and resewing. The entire process is repeated until the desired geometric design is created. This vest, in blue, green, and white, is an intricate example of Seminole patchwork. (For patchwork see chapter 6.)

The design, stenciled in brown and quilted, is the focal point of this vest. The fabric is cream-colored cotton, lined with a striped material in shades of brown, gold, and cream, which makes the garment reversible. Striped bias bands are used to trim the pockets, to outline the back motif, and to bind the edges.

Designer: Lois Ericson, model: Mike Ericson, photographer: Diane Ericson Frode

 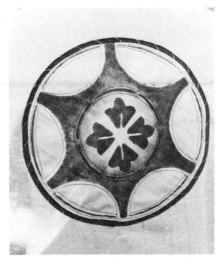

7. Japan

Japanese family crests became popular in the 11th century. The original designs were very intricate and were used on kimonos worn by members of the imperial court. Simplified designs were worn to identify warriors in battle. These motifs are still used but no longer necessarily represent a family name.

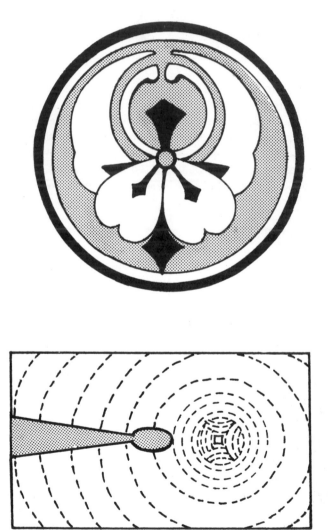

Satin was the fabric choice for this vest; maroon was the basic color, with cream bias bands and a lovely blue medallion. The circular design is a copy of a Japenese family crest. The machine stitching emphasizes the lines in the composition. The vest has a plain neckline with no fasteners and square armholes. The rust-colored cotton vest also displays a family crest, this one a coin motif. A large piece of fabric was quilted with a circular design at one end, and concentric circles were sewn around it. The vest was then cut out and folded at the shoulder seams. The lines form a rounded pattern when fastened in the middle. The vest reverses to a printed cotton.

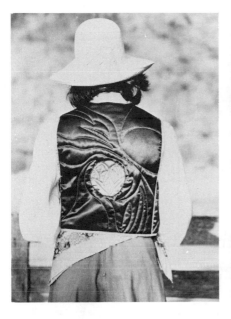

Designer/photographer: Heidi Hybl, model: Suzi Lofaso

8. Greece

This sleeveless tunic for women comes from the area around Athens. The off-white unlined surcoat is made of thick felted wool and embroidered with dark brown wool and variegated blue silk thread. The strips sewn near the neckline at the front edges are made of brocade fabric. To add fullness at the lower edge, a gusset is inserted on the side seams.

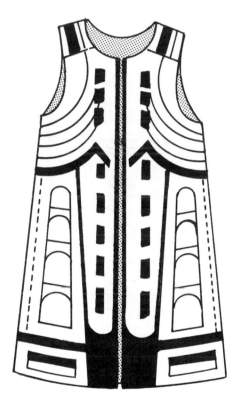
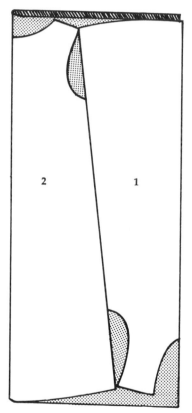

1 front   2 back

This vest had a very elegant beginning as the quilted lining of a cashmere coat made in Hong Kong. The designer came across it at a secondhand store. The cream-colored silk-satin lining pieces were taken apart and individually relined with burgundy cotton satin. The side seams were faggoted together with a feather stitch. The neck edge waist. Very loose, baggy pants complete the outfit.
emphasized with running stitches in dark red thread.

Designer/model: Lois Ericson,
photographer: Diane Ericson Frode

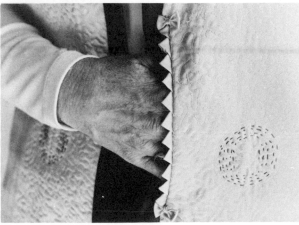

9. Kurdistan

This is an unusual sleeveless jacket made of heavy felted, woven woolen material. The edges are placed side by side and sewn together. The narrow fabric was creased in the middle while it was made. Under the vest a ramie shirt with long pointed sleeves is worn. If the sleeves get in the way, the ends are buttoned behind the neck or wrapped around the waist. Very loose, baggy pants completes the outfit.

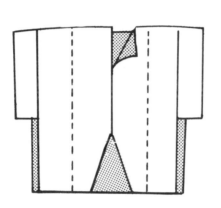

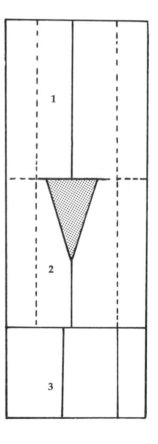

1 back   2 front   3 side panels

102

The designs on these two appliquéd vests were inspired by the south-western desert area. The fabric is a cotton-polyester blend. The colors are muted yet lively, as only the desert can be. The appliqués are sewn by hand, and a simple tie fastens the front together.

Designer: Jo Diggs, model: Valerie Currier, photographer: Tim Rotroff

10. Germany

In the 16th century sleeveless doublets were popular. This one, which comes from Germany, was made of intricately stitched wine-colored velvet. The shoulder seams, armholes, center front, and lower hem were decorated with an elegant braid. Short padded breeches and a long-sleeved shirt with lace trim and ruff were worn with the vest. Matching wine stockings and a short cream-colored cape completed this fashionable attire.

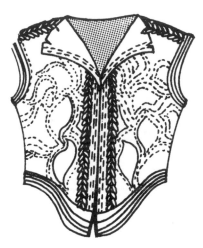

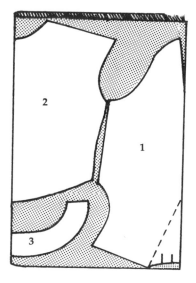

1 front   2 back   3 armhole facing

Designer/model: Diane Ericson Frode, photographer: Chas Frode

A cotton scarf from Japan forms the decorative element of this vest. The scarf has a yellow background; the figure is in black and green, with a dusty-rose fan. The scarf is piped in the rose color. The appliqués on the front panels are made of plum silk and dull jade-green cotton. The yoke and back are of black-and-cream-striped silk. The vest is lined with a dark plum-colored rayon fabric, and the edges are bound with black and green silk bias strips. The closures are made from two old oriental coins, held in place by the stitched ties.

Purple, mauve, and fuchsia combine beautifully in this vest. An art-nouveau design is stenciled in purple on mauve at the lower edge. (See chapter 6 for stenciling instructions.) The design was quilted lightly, and the running stitches add interest and make the hem firm. The armholes are finished with fuchsia bias bands. The button loops and knot buttons are made of corded bias tubing. (See chapter 6 for corded-tubing instructions.)

Designer/model: Lois Ericson, photographer: Diane Ericson Frode

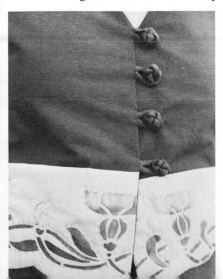
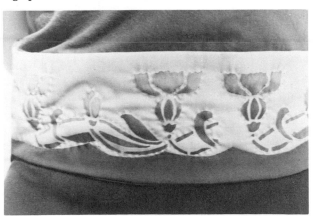

11. Arabia

This short, sleveless coat worn by mountain men in Arabia, was made of skins. The fur side was turned in for warmth, while the smooth side was embroidered and appliquéd with small pieces of red leather for decoration. A rolled leather button fastened the garment across the chest.

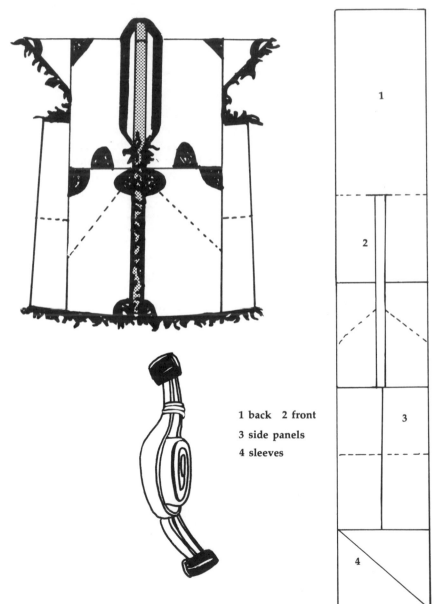

1 back   2 front
3 side panels
4 sleeves

The main body of this vest is made of heavy red brushed-cotton denim, with appliqués of Guatemalan cottons and Japanese materials such as machine-woven ikat. The colors are blue, red, yellow, and white, dramatically highlighted with black trim. The vest is lightly padded and both hand- and machine-quilted. (See chapter 6 for quilting directions.) The edges and seams are handsomely finished with satin and rayon-cotton ribbon and silk bias tape.

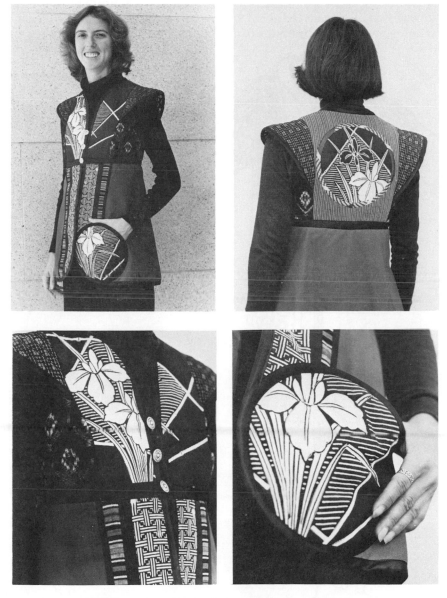

Designer: Nancy Love, photographer: Hannah Tandeta

12. Germany

In addition to the tabard a surcoat was also worn over suits of armor or chain mail. This particular one is from Germany, but this type of garment was popular throughout Europe from the 13th to the 15th centuries. Many variations of neckline, diagonal or front closing, and length were found. The one static feature was the immense armholes, which usually reached to the hips. From a rather plain beginning the surcoat was eventually adopted by women and made of very elegant materials, with wide fur bands trimming the neck, armholes, and hems.

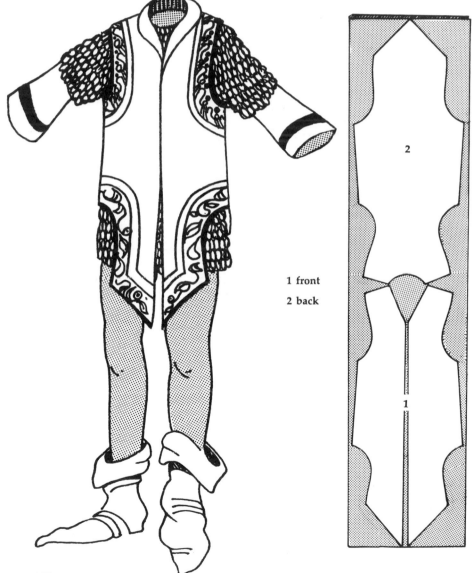

1 front

2 back

This surcoat or vest is made of a plum-colored linenlike fabric with a teal-blue cotton lining. Several prints were used to emphasize the armholes and the unusual side vents. These bands are appliquéd by hand. The vest has a detachable hood that is also lined with the teal-blue fabric.

Designer/model: Lois Ericson,
photographer: Diane Ericson Frode

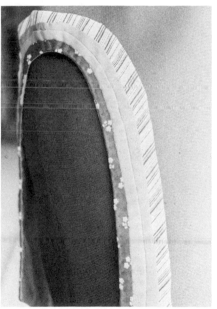

13. Sweden

In nearly all the European countries vests were worn as part of the national costume. This one, from Sweden, was worn with a white blouse and a silver brooch. The blouse was sometimes accordion-pleated by wrapping in damp muslin and heat-setting in a cooling oven. A wool skirt, fancy apron, elegant hat, and colored stockings completed the outfit. The vest usually buttoned or laced with cord and ornate silver loops. It was usually made of wool or linen and might be quilted, felted, or trimmed with braid, lace, or embroidery.

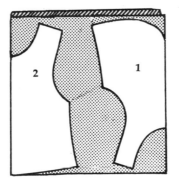

1 front   2 back

This blue cotton vest is trimmed with red, blue, and yellow appliquéd flowers once removed from an old tablecloth. The appliqués were reembroidered and accentuated with running stitches. The vest is lined with yellow cotton.

Designer/model: Kristine Barrett, photographer: Lois Ericson

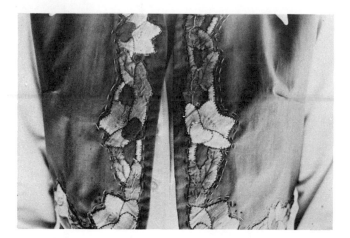

14. China

This vest from China has a vertical front closing, the influence of Mongolian styles. The blue cotton garment was worn by officials and soldiers. The circular lettered piece in the center is made of varnished shirting.

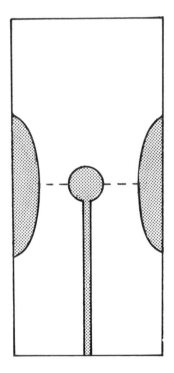

Brown cotton velveteen was the choice for this vest, which is lined with polyester crepe. The shoulder seams were sewn together on both the vest and the lining. The entire garment was lined at the same time, leaving a small opening for turning to the right side, which was then sewn together. The side seams were faggoted together—or ties could also be used to fasten the sides. The embroidery, in simple chain and running stitches, was done in such a way that the circle closes when the garment is worn.

Designer/model: Lois Ericson, photographer: Diane Ericson Frode

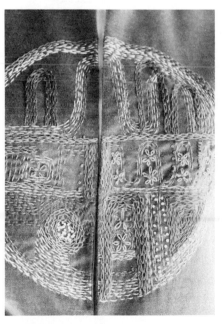

15. Brazil

This jerkin, called an *iccima* in South America, was worn by natives in battle. It was made of jaguar skins or woven aloe fiber. The back was made in one piece; the shoulder bands were extensions of the back. The front section was usually made in one piece, with no fastening of any kind.

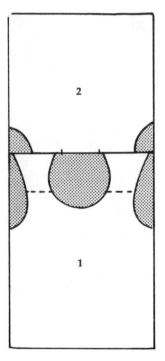

1 front   2 back

This vest is made of gray polyester knit with toast, black, and ecru embroidery. The art-nouveau flower is done in chain stitch. The direction of the stitches seems to shade the design in color. The tunic is simply cut, with a round neck and cap sleeves.

Designer/model: Linda Edison, photographer: B. Johnson

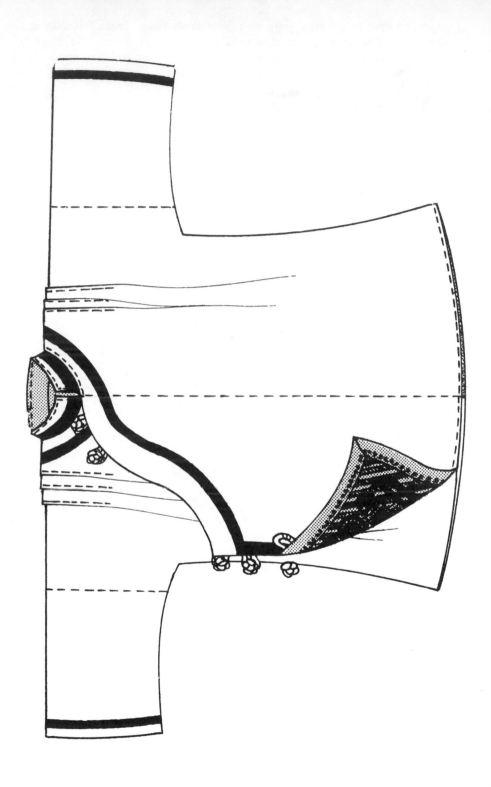

CHAPTER IV.

The Jacket

During the reign of the French king Louis XIV, outside pockets for garments were first introduced on the fashion scene.

1. Spain

The *mandilion*, a Spanish jacket from the 16th century, was a popular garment that was worn around the shoulders as a cape. This sleeved doublet was close-fitting and made of spring-green velvet. The metal buttons and loops were placed very close together, making the front very decorative. Slashes in the fabric to show the lining or undergarment were common during the Renaissance. The ruff, worn by both men and women, was a detachable collar, usually made of fine linen or cotton. It was starched very stiff and came in various widths, using up to 18 yards of narrow fabric. The large folding hood, which was hooped with whalebone, is called a *calash*, after the folding top of a light carriage with the same name. It was popular around 1770 and was revived in 1820. This style of hood protected the women's high coiffures that were prevalent in those two periods.

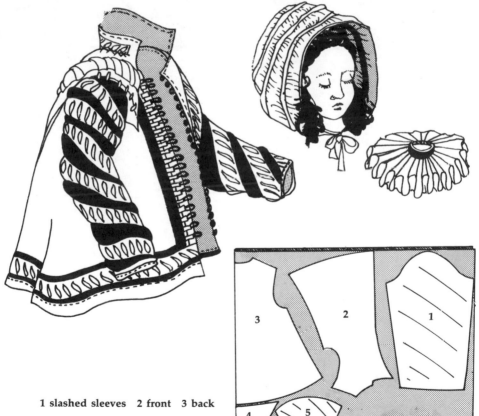

1 slashed sleeves 2 front 3 back
4 collar 5 shoulder ornament

The materials and techniques used to make this jacket were chosen to simulate the original costume. The crocheted ribbon accentuates the fullness and texture of the slashed *mandilion* sleeve. The chamois softens the shape of the bodice front and the back yoke. The raffia takes on the rigid character of the *calash*. Human hair, raw fleece, and elastic represent the jeweled embellishments. The design of the woven raffia suggests the pattern of the original fabric. This garment, made in rich natural colors, is a very free interpretation of an ethnic style.

Designer/model: Andrea Woynick,
photographer: James Cook

2. Wales

This smock from Wales was usually made of gray cotton or linen fabric. It was a "workshirt" worn by country folk. It was long, reaching roughly to the knees, and was worn with pants and a black hat with a round crown and wide brim. The garment had a front yoke, with set-in straight sleeves and a narrow standup collar. The shirt buttoned partway down in front.

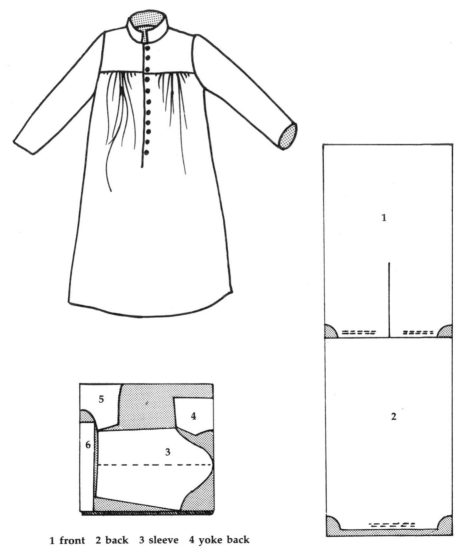

1 front 2 back 3 sleeve 4 yoke back
5 yoke front 6 collar

Strip patchwork was the technique used to make this colorful jacket. The 1" strips were cut from polyester-cotton fabric. The accent colors are blue, orange, green, and off-white, with plum as the main color. The lining and strips were all sewn at one time. (See chapter 6 for details on strip patchwork.) The plain front bands and small stand-up collar could be lightly padded if desired.

Designer/model: Lois Ericson, photographer: Diane Ericson Frode

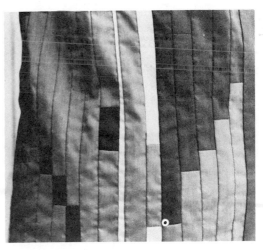

3. France

The tunics of 15th-century France were adopted by nearly all the other European countries, particularly Spain, Germany, and Italy. France even then was the fashion trendsetter. This doublet was a very practical garment, worn by the nobleman's head falconer. The leather sleeves made a perfect perch for the birds. The bodice was also made of leather to protect the falconer as he rode through heavy underbrush in search of fallen game. To complete the costume, long hose and soft shoes with pointed toes were worn. The shoes were sometimes eliminated, and the soles were sewn directly onto the hose.

1 front   2 back   3 sleeve   4 short sleeve
5 padded shoulder piece   6 collar

This handsome leather-and-crochet tunic could have stepped directly out of an old costume book. The tobacco-brown suede that forms the main body of the garment is handsewn together on the sides, shoulder, and sleeves. The upper sleeves, collar, and center front are crocheted of handspun natural-dyed yarns. The colors are forest green, brown, gold, and orange, combined with icy blue rayon cord. The interesting closure is a button-loop frog with a copper tube in the middle. (See chapter 6 for crochet directions.)

Designer/model: Alix Peshette,
photographer: Libby Harmor

4. Manchuria

This dress from Manchuria was made of dyed or painted fish skins (what a challenge!), which were pieced together. The appliqué border and hemline designs were made of dyed deerskins. The lower edge of the tunic was lined with fine cotton, and the sleeves were faced with red flannel. The cording at the neck edge is black velvet.

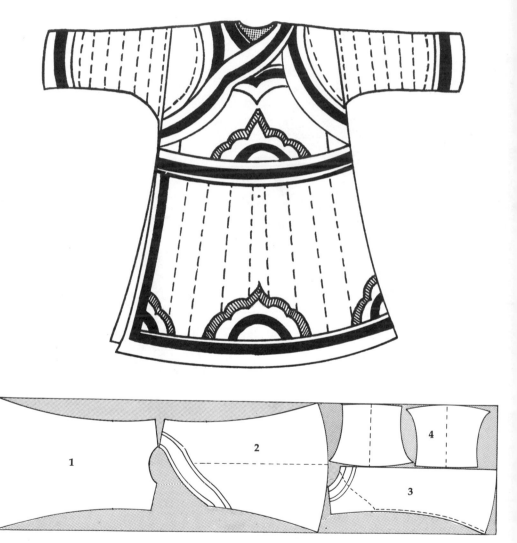

1 back   2 left front   3 right front   4 sleeve

These two jackets show a Manchurian inspiration in their quilted appearance, shaped sleeves, and general feeling. These bold interpretations are made of natural cotton with blue and brown appliqué. The appliquéd pieces are machine-quilted to the background fabric. The filler and lining are sewn at the same time.

Designer: Nancy Gano,
model: Linda Collins,
photographer: Friedolin Kessler

5. China

The Orient has had great influence on fashion for hundreds of years. This simple unlined coat made of blue-gray silk is called a *ha'ol*. The fabric is pieced very artistically—all Chinese garments have a center front and back seams. Note the little pocket under the front panel. There is a traditional button-and-loop closing.

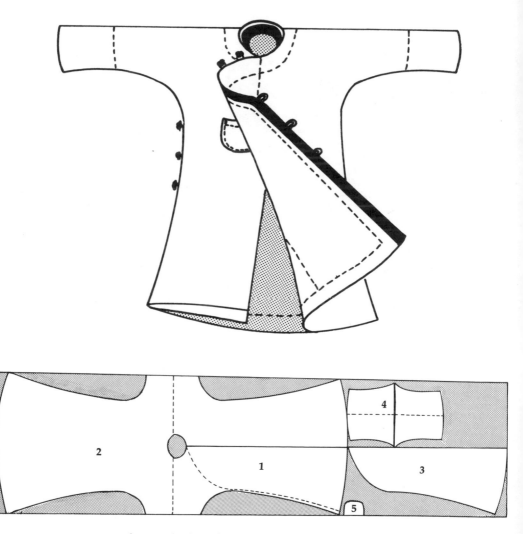

1 front   2 back   3 front lap panel   4 sleeves   5 pocket

This short-sleeved jacket is made from an old 1930s quilt. The oriental style was chosen to take advantage of the "Grandmother's Flower Garden" design without overcutting. The buttons are made of mother-of-pearl and fasten with loops. The jacket is unlined but is faced with muslin. The quilt was quite worn, so parts of the design had to be reappliquéd.

Designer/photographer: Joanne Purpus, model: Leslie Suzuki

6. England

This 14th-century English tunic was worn by a page, the son of a well-to-do family who was sent to live with a nobleman. The page, in return for various duties, was educated with the nobleman's children. The uniform was short, with notched hem and sleeve edges, and was usually made of bright colors. It was worn with a plain skirt, tights, and pointed soft shoes.

1 front 2 back 3 capelike yoke
4 capelike front and back
5 front tab 6 back facing 7 sleeve
8 skirt front 9 skirt back

This tunic features yellow as the main color, with accents of dark purple and red. It was completely woven of wool yarns in a pin-weaving technique. (Pin weaving is discussed in chapter 6.) All the hems were finished as the garment was taken off the cardboard. The sleeves and sides were fastened with a braid made of yellow and red yarn.

Designer/model: P.J. Walton, photographer: Gregg Palmer

7. Burma

This Burmese woman's coat is made of fine cream-colored wool. It is decorated with flowered-calico and plain strips on the center front and sleeve bands. These cotton bands are also used as the facings on the side slits. Bronze clasps fasten the front closures.

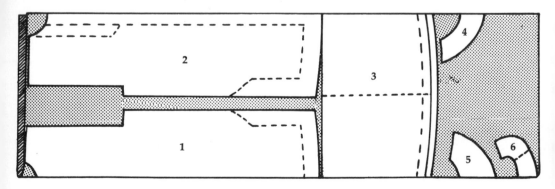

1 back   2 front   3 sleeve   4 front facing   5 back facing   6 collar

A rust-colored ribbed acrylic knit is combined with various cotton prints to make this handsome jacket. These are two large patch pockets on each side of the front. The seams are turned to the outside and stitched so that the linging covers the raw edges. The edges of this lining are turned under and hand-stitched to finish. Small ties fasten the front. Even the hood is lined, making this garment reversible.

Designer/model: Diane Ericson Frode, photographer: Chas Frode

8. Iran

This Iranian outer garment from the 19th century was directly patterned after an antique Iranian cloak. It is cut in one piece. BF is cut and folded on the dotted lines for the neck opening. The shoulder line is folded so that AB on one side and BC on the other match the side parts and is sewn together. The sleeves are sewn together and decorated with colored embroidery similar to that on the neck edge.

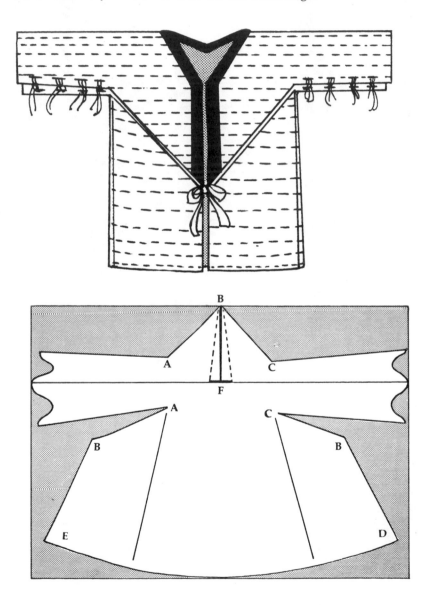

The cotton material is machine-quilted, and all the cut edges are bound with bias tape. The appliquéd shapes are outlined with machine-stitched satin stitch. When the jacket is reversed, the design forms a very subtle outline, a very effective use of shapes. The main colors of this jacket are red, white, blue, and pink. The underarm sleeve section ties together in the same manner as in front.

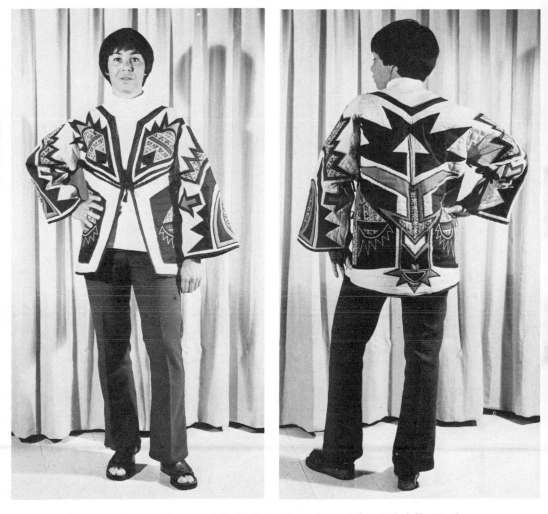

Designer: Nancy Gano, model: Linda Collins, photographer: Friedolin Kessler

9. Turkey

A *djubbeh* is an overcoat worn over a caftan that originated in Turkey and Asia Minor. The back is cut in several diagonal pieces, which are sewn to a large triangular piece in the center. The sleeves are narrow and set into a square armhole. The front panels overlap and fasten with a button at the plain neck edge. This garment is seldom lined—if it is lined, a quiet color of silk is used. The most popular colors for the *djubbeh* were wine red, brown, gray, and blue.

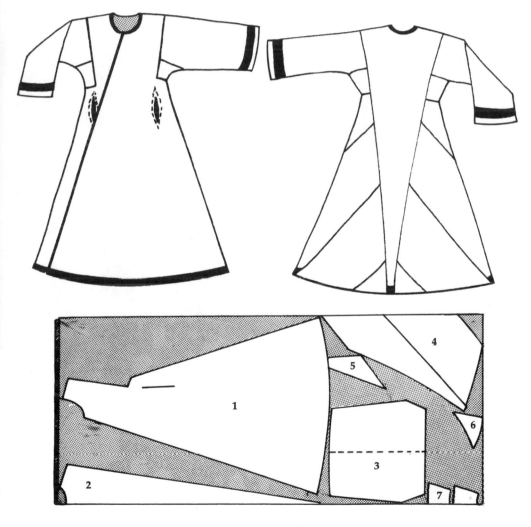

1 front   2 back   3 sleeve   4, 5, 6 side back pieces   7 gussets

This hand-quilted evening jacket, patterned after a man's *djubbeh*, is made of teal-blue velveteen. The sleeves are pin-woven of fine wool yarns. The principal colors are black, white, and blue, accented with rust-colored chenille and fluffs of unspun fleece. (Pin weaving is explained in chapter 6.)

Designer/model: Maureen Boggs, photographer: Diane Ericson Frode

10. Manchuria

This jacket from Manchuria is made of diagonally woven bright red cotton. The back is in one piece but has a slit up to the waist. The front is fastened with buttons and loops. A very similar style is worn in the People's Republic of China, but a set-in sleeve, patch pockets, and drab colors are used.

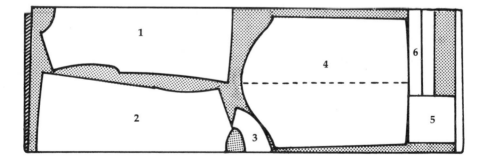

1 front   2 back   3 collar   4 sleeves   5 pocket   6 ties

This jacket is made of silk recycled from old dresses from India. The collar and sleeve stripes are made of patchwork. The appliquéd and embroidered butterfly was inspired by the freedom that this insect enjoys. The quilting lines, border, and back design signify water, a dominant element in the artist's life. The main color in this jacket is lavender, with dark blue borders. The appliqués and patchwork are done in several shades of blue, green, and purple.

Designer/model: Cindy Van Dine, photographer: Barbara Alves

11. Turkey

In the 17th century the *mente* was a popular coatlike tunic. It was simply cut, with wide sleeves, narrow collar, and frogged fastenings. The front panels and sleeve bands were richly embroidered with silver and gold thread. The fabrics were brocades and silks in elegant colors. Flared top boots, colored hose, and a fur-trimmed hat completed the outfit.

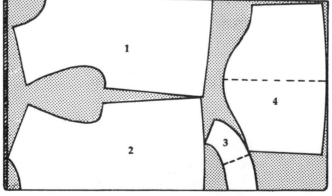

1 front   2 back   3 collar   4 sleeve

The simple construction of the Turkish *mente* prompted this short jacket made of polyester-cotton fabric. The pages of a 1905 child's cloth book on horses were appliquéd on the material. The garment was hand- and machine-quilted, and bias bands were used to finish the edges. The colors of the jacket are beige, tobacco, off-white, pale green, and dark red. One of the pages of the book shows an Indian prince riding an Arabian horse.

Designer/model: Lois Ericson,
photographer: Diane Ericson Frode

12. Turkey

This Turkish woman's shirt was made of striped cotton. The cut of this tunic is very original, with one piece of fabric extending from the undersleeve down the sides and connecting the front and back. The collar buttons to the shirt, and the sleeve hems and front edge are finished with crochet.

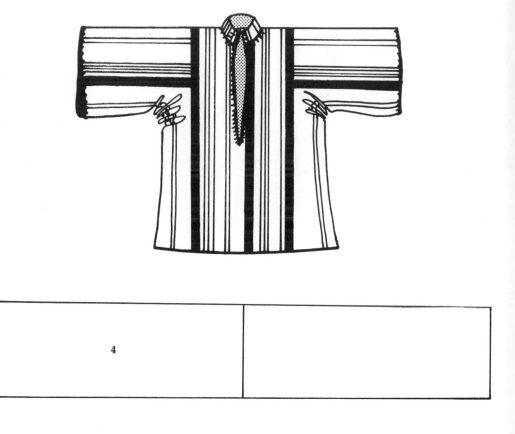

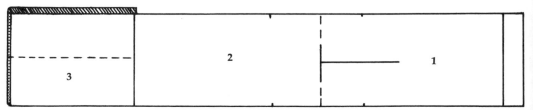

1 front   2 back   3 oversleeves   4 undersleeves

A short-sleeved jacket done in the strip-patchwork technique is effective in black and brown. The jacket is underlined; the strips are sewn to it; and the garment is lined. Slit pockets are set in the side-front seams. Narrow bands finish the sleeve edges and hem. Bone toggle buttons and loops form the closures.

Designer/photographer: Joanne Purpus, model: Leslie Suzuki

13. Mexico

This full shirt from Mexico was made of handloomed cotton. The color was usually white to reflect the heat and fit loosely for added comfort. On the bodice the material was gathered onto a narrow neckband. Ties or knotted buttons (see chapter 6) and loops were sometimes used at the neck as fasteners. The sleeves are straight in this example, although they could also be full and gathered onto a band, as at the neck edge.

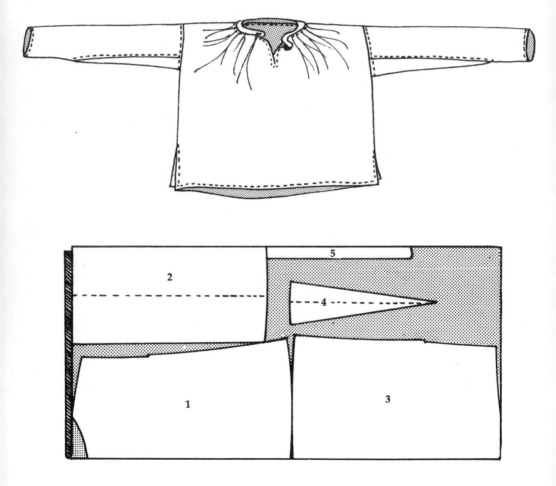

1 front   2 sleeve   3 back   4 gusset   5 neckband

Fabric is only one possibility for making a tunic. In this example the pieces of the shirt are crocheted, resulting in a beautiful one-of-a-kind sweater. It is very heavy and easily wards off rain and cold. The design motifs are inspired by ancient bird patterns from Colima. These motifs were very often used as stamps to decorate the body. How fitting it is that they once again are used to adorn the body! Dog-hair and hand-spun wool yarns in natural colors, some dyed with onionskins, are used. (See chapter 6 for crochet instructions.)

Designer/model: Alix Peshette, photographer: Libby Harmor

14. Iraq

Jackets from Iraq were usually made of cotton, either in plain dark colors or in bright stripes. The pear-shaped buttons were covered with fabric and fastened with cord loops. The edges of the pockets, sleeves, and neck were also trimmed with silk cord. Plain-colored jackets were often embroidered and had inside pockets that were also handsomely embroidered (a little something for the wearer to enjoy personally—"flowers for the soul," as they say).

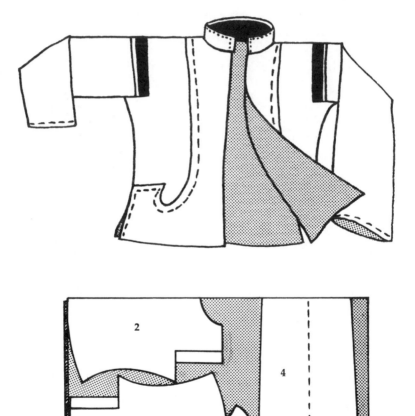

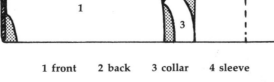

1 front   2 back   3 collar   4 sleeve

Designer/model: Pat Goldstene,
photographer: Paul Goldstene

Designer/model: Lois Ericson,
photographer: Diane Ericson Frode

This jacket is made entirely of felt, which makes appliquéing fairly easy—no edges to turn under and no raveling seams to finish. The scene on the jacket depicts an old western town complete with general store, hotel, and jail. This design idea could be used with many scenes from childhood—from a favorite painting or a lunar landscape—perfect for a child's garment. After the pieces were cut out and appliquéd to the jacket, the embroidery was added to accentuate the shapes and heighten the "realism."

The fabric for this jacket was originally used in a heavy cotton embroidered skirt from Afhganistan. It is dark red, with white, yellow, green, and black needle-woven designs used on the allover pattern as well as on the border. An appliquéd dark gray band of felt is also machine-stitched to the edge of the border. The jacket was cut to utilize the border, which originally circled the bottom of the skirt. The buttons are very old silver disks.

145

15. Japan

This 16th-century chief's costume from Japan was made of thin bark woven on primitive looms. The warp was cotton, usually set up to create a stripe effect. The cotton patchwork on the hems and sleeves was embroidered in a scroll design. The dark blue appliqués on the yellow background were quite effective.

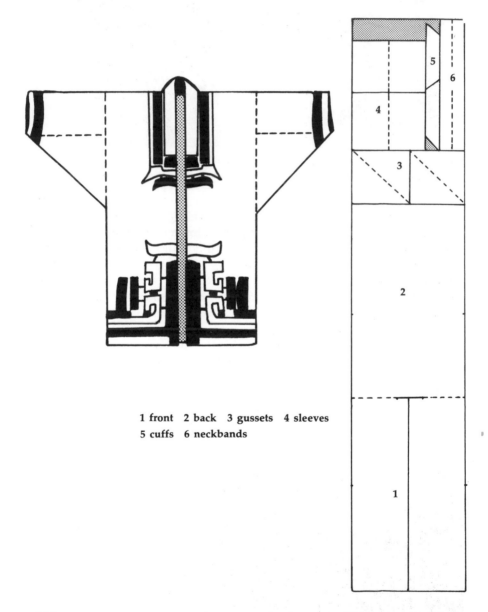

1 front   2 back   3 gussets   4 sleeves
5 cuffs   6 neckbands

The oriental cut of this jacket is enhanced by the black gabardine fabric. The striped rayon materials in shades of black, rust red, green, and gray are from Japan. They are cut in simple shapes and hand-appliquéd to the shoulder and back areas. The cut of this comfortable jacket is equally flattering to men or women. The front fastens with stitched ties.

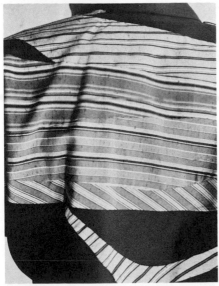

Designer: Lois Ericson,
model: Lennart Ericson,
photographer: Diane Ericson Frode

16. Korea

In Korea the colors emphasize the various stages of life. Children wear very bright colors; after marriage white in combination with soft pastel colors is allowed. All-white costumes are the privilege of the old. This woman's jacket is made of heavy pink cotton lined with fine white cotton. Jackets cut in this style and made of embroidered silk are worn for special occasions.

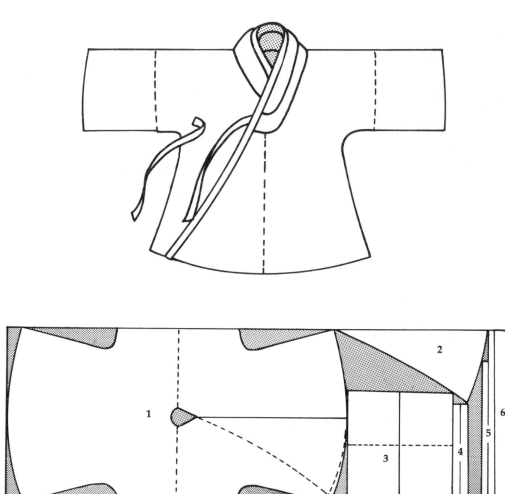

1 front and back   2 front flap   3 sleeves   4 ties   5 front band trim   6 collar

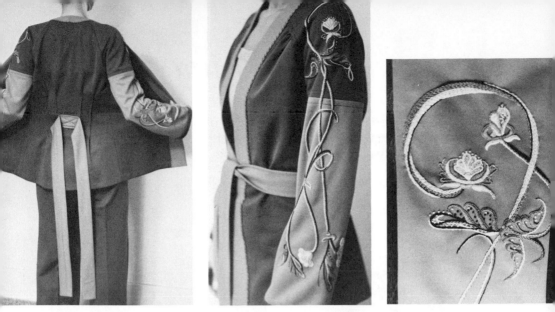

Designer/model: Linda Edison, photographer: B. Johnson

Mauve- and plum-colored knits are the basic fabrics used in this un-lined jacket. The embroidery on the sleeves is a floral design executed in feather and chain stitches with french-knot accents. The sleeve design is done in lavender, mauve, purple, gold, and peach. The belt fastens in the center back with decorative stitching. A bias band finishes the neck and front edges.

This toast-colored cotton jacket incorporates appliqués of old-fashioned hand puppets. They were padded and stitched in place. Green and black embroidery accents emphasize the shapes of the dolls and the lines of the garment.

Designer/model: Kristine Barrett, photographer: Lois Ericson

17. China

This jacket belonged to a Chinese soldier of high rank. The fabric was silk brocade, underlined with heavy cotton. It was decorated with gold paillettes, similar to armor, for protection. The edges were decorated with velvet and silk cording. The colors of this elegant jacket were shades of purple, blue, and green with black.

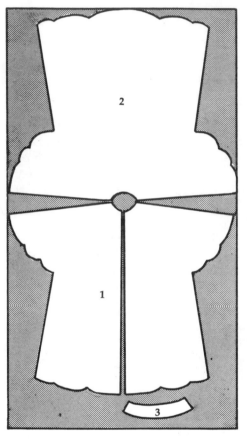

1 front   2 back   3 collar

This jacket was woven in four pieces, matching the designs on the sides, front, and back. The overall design was not the same on each piece—the colored shapes flow into one another. The pieces were underlined and sewn together on the shoulders. To reemphasize the shapes, silk and rayon embroidery was added. The garment was lined with lime and wine fabric. The neck, sleeve edges, and hems were finished with bands of wine-colored velveteen. An antique buckle decorates the front closure. Loops and buttons fasten the sides together. The colors of this jacket are red, wine, rust, lavender, fuchsia, and a touch of lime green. The detail shows how the woven shapes are accentuated by the embroidery.

Designer/model:
Lois Ericson,
photographer:
Diane Ericson Frode

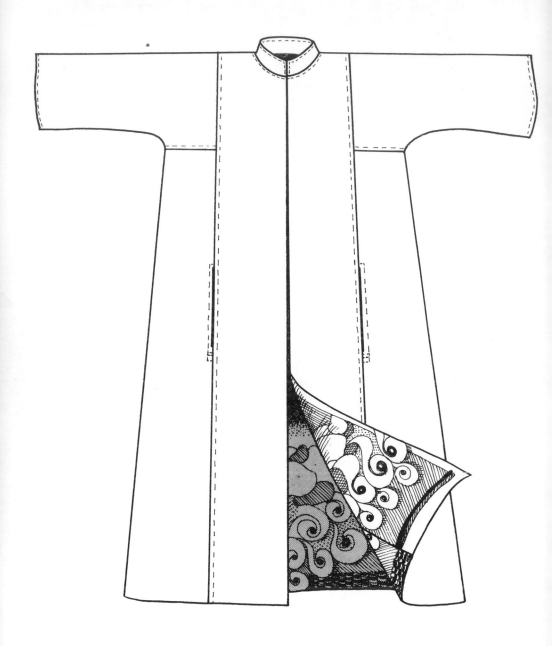

CHAPTER V.

The Coat

The Persians were the first culture to cut and fit garments. In the 6th century B.C. they introduced the coat with fitted, sewn-in sleeves.

1. Persia

Most of the Middle Eastern countries have some form of the caftan. This long-sleeved garment, usually made of cotton, was put together from a series of embroidered panels. These panels were recycled so that, when new ones were added, the garments had an asymmetrical, individual quality. These caftans were very often dark blue or black, with gold and red-orange embroidery.

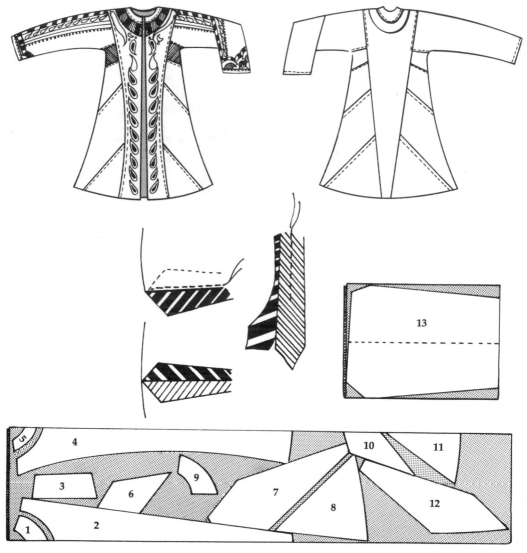

1 yoke back   2 back   3 underarmband   4 front   5 yoke front trim
6, 7, 8 back side pieces   9 yoke front   10, 11, 12 front side pieces   13 sleeve

This coat, an interpretation of the caftan, is made of blue denim, with appliqués or red, orange, light blue, and gold. The surface embellishments are made from striped neckties (a great recycling idea), grosgrain ribbon, and machine embroidery. The design medallions and striped sections were stitched in place, and the raw edges were covered with grosgrain ribbon. Each pattern piece was embellished separately before the garment was sewn together. The neckties were sewn in the seams to add to the design on the outside of the garment and to fold over and finish the seams on the inside. The machine embroidery was stitched from the wrong side of the denim with silk buttonhole twist on the bobbin.

Designer/model: Nancy Papa,
photographer: John Ridgely

155

2. Syria

This quilted man's coat comes from Syria. It was made of blue-gray satin and lined with cream-colored silk twill. The quilting design was done in vertical lines on the sleeves and main body of the tunic. The bands at the wrist, front edges, and hemline are quilted in a small diagonal pattern. The two underarm pieces combine a geometric scheme with abstract flowers.

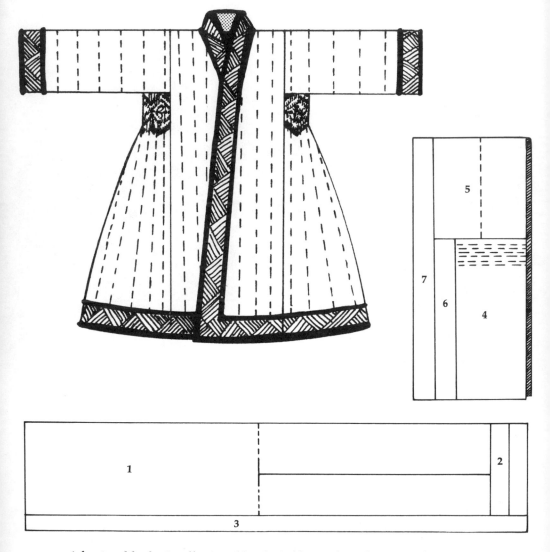

1 front and back   2 cuffs   3 neckband   4 side panel   5 sleeve   6, 7 hembands

The fabric for this coat is machine-quilted brushed denim in a warm rose-purple color. The quilted bands are navy blue cotton, with a narrower band of rust for accent. There are pockets on each side in the side-front seams. Flowered voile was used as the lining.

Designer/model: Lois Ericson, photographer: Diane Ericson Frode

3. China

This classic oriental style was made of ice-blue silk with a peach lining. The contrasting bands, piping, and knot buttons were made of gray satin. An indigo-blue sleeveless coat or short vest was worn over this robe. China retained the secret of silk making until the 6th century A.D. when silkworms were smuggled out of China in a princess' headdress (or so the tale is told).

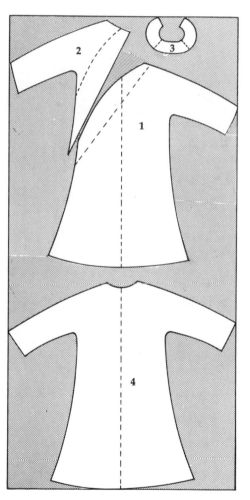

1 left front   2 right front

3 collar   4 back

This purple velvet evening coat was inspired by a Chinese emperor's coat from the Ch'ing Dynasty. The elegant brocades from Japan and Nepal, used for facings, bias cord, and lower sleeves, are in two shades of blue. Light bias cording is used on the dark blue, and dark blue on the light. The glass buttons placed diagonally across the front are also from Nepal. The collar is recycled old lace. On the back of the tunic is a subtle beaded design.

Designer/model:
Cindy Van Dine,
photographer:
Barbara Alves

4. India

This coat from Kashmir, India was made of green cashmere wool. The striped designs were done in couched gold cord. The lining was raspberry and green taffeta. Crimson and white striped silk trousers and a turban with black heron feathers completed the outfit.

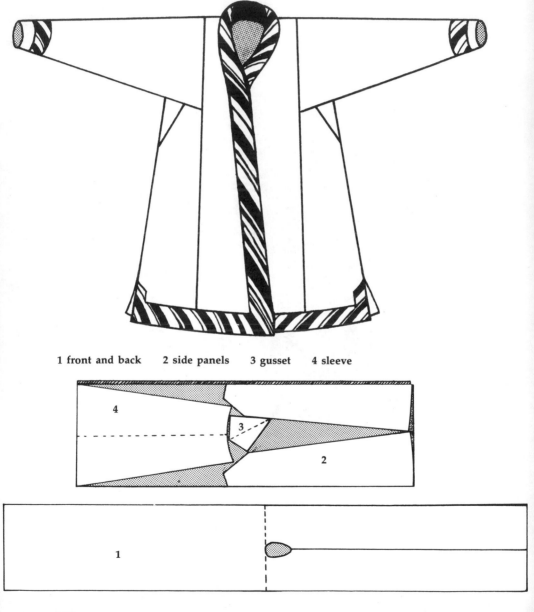

1 front and back   2 side panels   3 gusset   4 sleeve

This coat has wide beige sleeves and side panels. The front panels are tie-dyed in shades of brown and rust. The bands at the front edges and hems are batiked in yellow, orange, and brown. Handmade glass buttons and loops complete the diagonal closing.

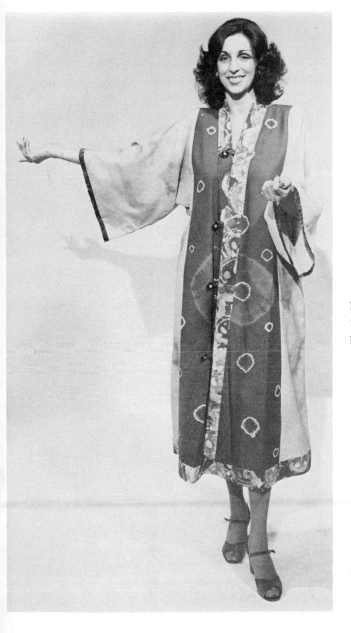

Designer: Anna Polesny,
model: Beverly Rohe,
photographer: Greg Mayhood

5. Africa

This tunic once belonged to a warrior from central Sudan. Blue designs are appliquéd on natural-colored cotton fabric; embroidered bands decorate the neck and waist. Several pockets held protective charms.

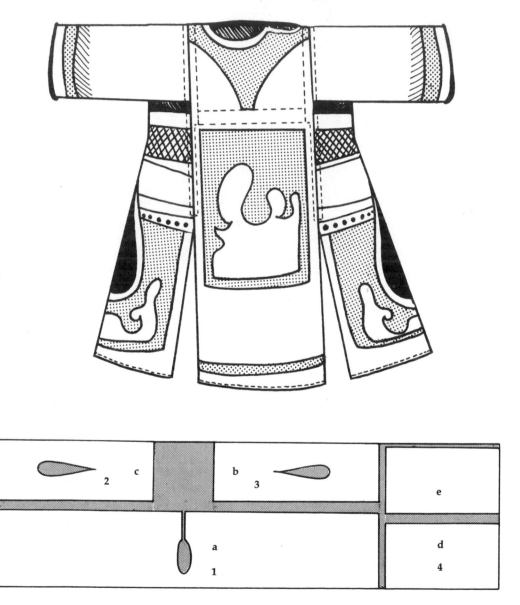

1 front and back center panel   2, 3 side panels   4 sleeves

French vanilla and chocolate are the colors of this coat. The fabric is a slubbed rayon-cotton blend. Four sections were woven, two for the front and back and two for the sides (with planned slits for the pockets). All the fabric shapes were quilted in a geometric pattern, except for the woven panels, which were sewn. Quilting was the perfect solution to the problem of balancing the heavy look of the woven panels. The panels on the "skirt" swing freely—a small strip of fabric was sewn underneath to simulate a pleat. The detail shows a closeup of the of brown, rust, and natural woven panel.

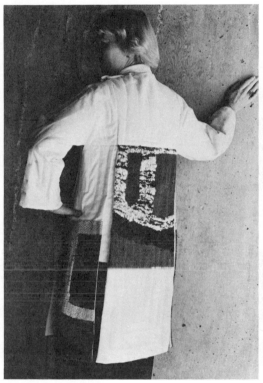

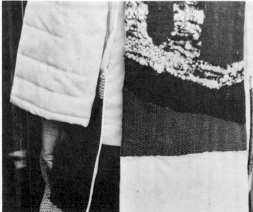

Designer/model: Lois Ericson,
photographer: Diane Ericson Frode

163

6. Turkey

This Turkish ceremonial coat, called an *usth-kurby*, was worn by the Sultan and other men of high rank. It was a popular style in the 16th to the 19th centuries. The seam was left open from the shoulder to the waist so the caftan-covered arms could extend. The fabrics used were white velvet and gold and green silk, often trimmed with sable.

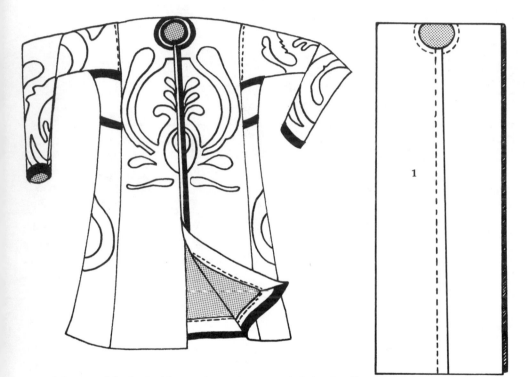

1 front and back   2 side panels   3 sleeves   4 belt (optional)

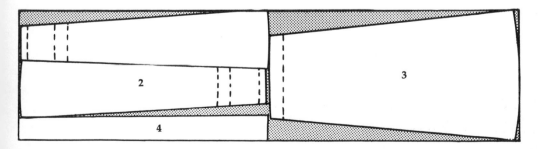

This elegant evening coat is aptly named *Coat of Diamonds.* It is made of gold satin, with red satin diamonds inset in the seams, neckline, sleeves, and slit center back. All the hems carry out the design with a sawtoothed edge. Slit pockets are included in the princess seaming used for the side-front panels. The closures are red glass ball buttons and loops. The lining is red and gold striped satin.

Designer/model: Perri Kimono, photographer: Jeorgia Anderson

7. *Japan*

The kimono is a graceful and elegant garment from Japan. The sleeves are set at right angles to the body and serve as pockets. Women's kimonos incorporate very beautiful patterns and often have padded hemlines. Silk and/or rayon are the usual fabrics, although cotton is also popular, especially for men. Kimonos are taken taken apart completely for laundering, then sewn back together again. They are expected to last for three generations. The obi is the most important accessory. This sash, usually 1' wide and up to 13' long, is wound around the waist and fastened. It is made of colorful brocade.

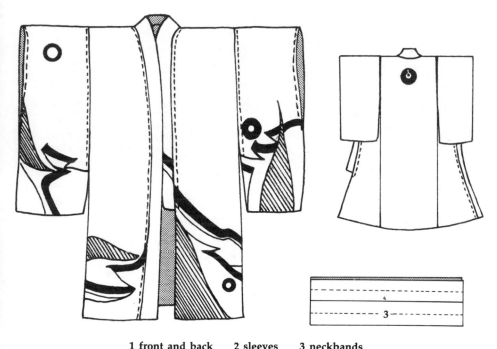

1 front and back   2 sleeves   3 neckbands

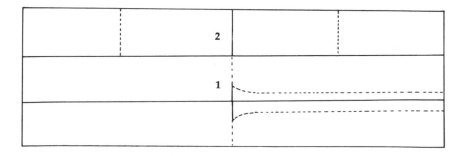

This handsome kimono is colored in shades of pink and rose cotton. Stylized flora and fauna designs display a distinct oriental influence. The detailed pieces are machine-appliquéd. The original obi sash is scaled down to a wrapped tie belt. The large piping at the bottom edge molds the border and gives weight and form to the hemline.

Designer/model: Nancy MacLeod, photographer: Robert McKenna

8. *Mongolia*

This blue dress of coarse cotton is from Mongolia. The borders and sleeve insets are silk, woven in a rainbow of colors. A shaped piece of wood covered with padded fabric keeps the shoulders and sleeve cap in place. The horse-hoof cuffs cover the hands or are folded back. The dress is lined with light blue silk and banded with red.

1 underarm   2 top back   3 left front
4 front waist inset   5 right front
6 bodice front band   7, 8 skirt back and front
9 collar   10 lower sleeve   11 upper sleeve

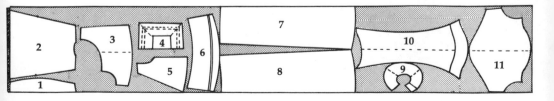

The "Buck Flash" satin coat is a delightful combination of oriental and space-age garb. The main body of the coat and the pants are in navy bluc. The inset stripes are yellow and red, with purple outlining the pattern pieces. The winglike shoulders cap a fitted appliquéd sleeve, which ends in a quilted horse-hoof cuff. The back has a slit with a loose panel underneath. Covered buttons and loops close the front and continue up the stand-up quilted collar.

Designer/model: Perri Kimono, photographer: Jeorgia Anderson

9. Arabia

From Arabia comes this *aba* with sleeves, which is made of white cotton with stripes of pale yellow silk. The sleeves are fastened to the main body of the garment with open drawn-thread work. Lavish embroidery with a flower motif decorates the front.

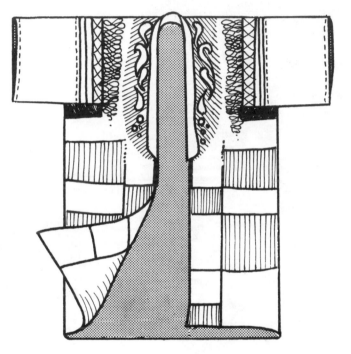

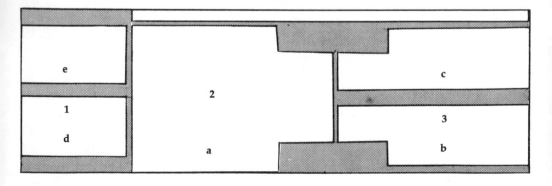

1 sleeves   2 back   3 front

This elegant evening coat is designed with separate panels that seem to float. The main body of the coat is woven with threads of fine linen, wool, and cotton. The sleeves and belt are crocheted; the embroidered trim is done with french knots and chain stitches. The art-nouveau buckle is silver, and the fabric colors are pale green, cream, maize, and touches of wine. The detail shows a closeup of the crocheted sleeves. There are no even rows or patterns to follow: single-crochet stitches are made until the shape of the sleeve is finished.

Designer/model: Lois Ericson,
photographer: Diane Ericson Frode

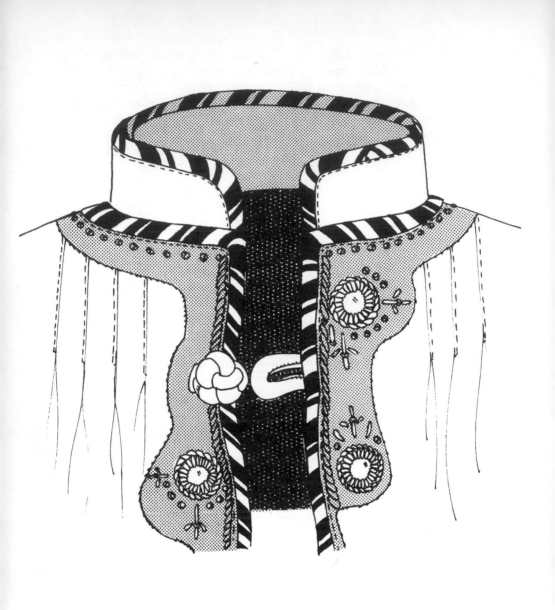

CHAPTER VI.

The Techniques

In 1914 a survey in New York City indicated that one-third of the family income was spent on the wife's wardrobe.

1. Tucks and Pleats

When tucks or pleats are desired on a garment, try this easy method. Instead of tedious marking machine-stitch the tucks on the fabric *first*, spacing them as you wish. This method works well with stripes and some colors can be made very prominent. The length of the fabric should be the same as the pattern piece; the width should be the width of the pattern piece plus 6" (more or less, depending on the fullness of the tucks or pleats).

a. Mark the center of the fabric.

b. Make tucks or pleats as you wish. Stitch in place or pin (if open pleats are made). Press.

c. Lay the pattern piece to be cut on the material, matching the center line to the center mark on the fabric. Cut out the pattern piece and continue as usual with the garment.

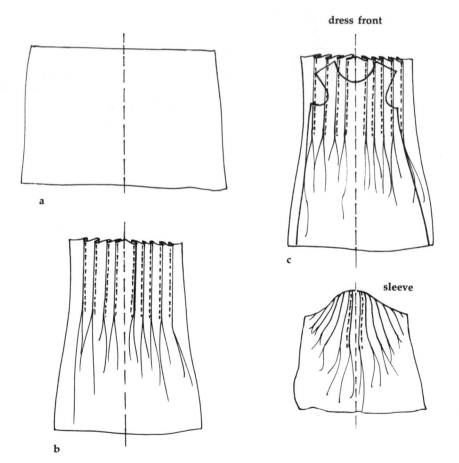

dress front

a

b

c

sleeve

174

2. Bias Binding

Follow this method to make bias binding.

a. Use a rectangular piece of fabric cut on the straight grain. Fold the fabric so the cut edge is parallel to the selvage; this fold is a true bias.

b. Cut on the fold and mark as many strips as needed. They should be twice the width plus 1/2" for the seam allowances.

c. Join the strips right sides together.

d. Press diagonal seams flat.

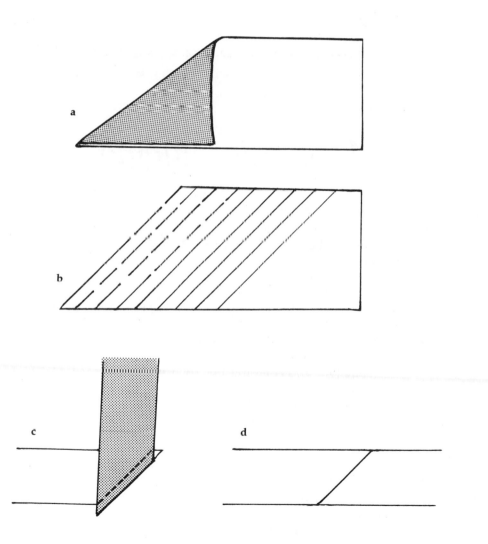

3. Corded Bias

Fold the bias right side out over the cording, leaving one side slightly wider than the other to avoid a bulky seam. Stitch close to the cord, using a zipper foot. Use a slightly larger stitch than you would normally use for the fabric. Machine chain stitch, if available, is the best choice.

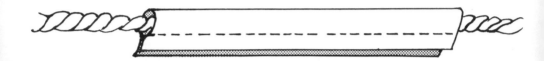

4. Corded Tubing

Here is how to make corded tubing.

a. Use cable cord twice the length of the bias strip and at least three times the width of the cord for the filler. Place the cord even with one end of the bias.

b. Fold the bias, with the right side towards the cording.

c. Stitch, using a zipper foot, and stretch the bias as you sew. At the end of the bias stitch across the cord, sewing the center of the cord to the bias strip.

d. Trim the seams close to the stitching.

e. Draw the end of the cord out of the bias, sliding the bias down, turning it inside out, and covering the other end of the cord. Trim off the excess cord.

f. The finished cord looks like this.

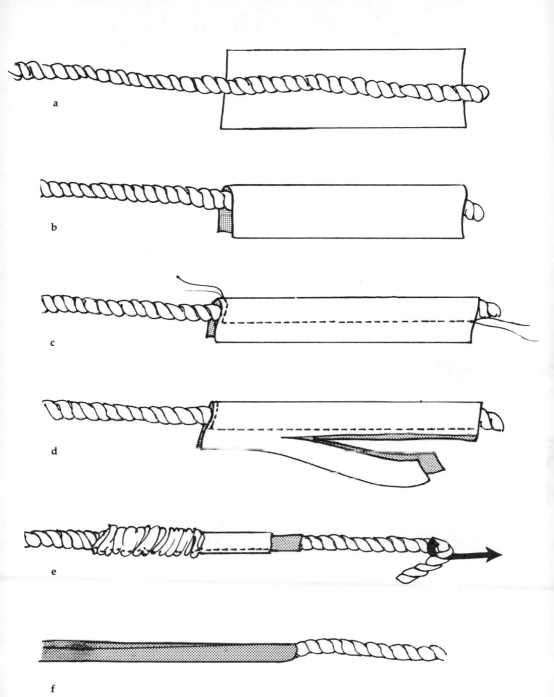

a

b

c

d

e

f

5. Corded Button Loops

Here is how to make corded button loops.

a. Baste a line for buttonhole placement.

b. Center a button on the line and form a loop around it with the cording to determine the correct size.

c. Cut the loops the length of the sample, space them on the line, and machine-baste in place.

d. Place the facing on the garment, right sides together, and stitch.

e. Trim the seams and turn. The seam allowance will lie flat if an additional line is stitched 1/4" from the seam on the facing side.

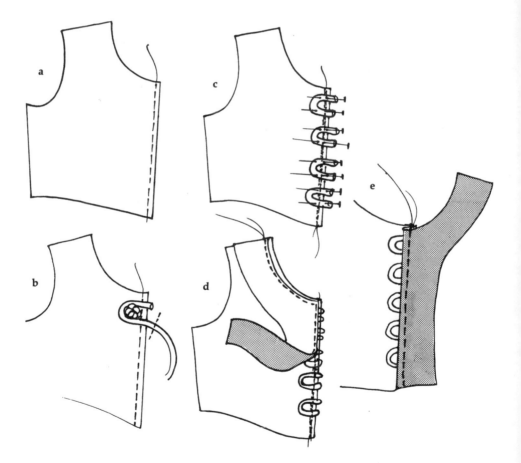

6. Chinese-knot Buttons

Use corded tubing or commercial cording. Cut a 15 " piece, possibly more if the cording is very thick.

a. Holding the first 2" in the left hand (if you are righthanded), make a counterclockwise loop over the tubing.

b. Holding the first loop, make another loop and place it underneath the first (like a pretzel). Follow the arrows to weave with the long end. This holds the loops together.

c. The finished loop pattern looks like this.

d. To tighten, draw up the loops carefully, working through with your fingers so that they are evenly tight.

e. Cut off the excess, leaving 1" on each end to fasten.

f. Whipstitch together.

g. The finished button looks like this.

Here is how to attach a knot button.

h. Sew it loosely to the fabric.

i. Fasten securely.

j. Wrap the thread around the stitches to make a shank.

k. The completed fastened button looks like this.

7. Mirror Embroidery

In addition to a shi-sha mirrors (see the list of suppliers) other materials can be used to give a similar effect. Circles can be cut from Mylar, a fabric-backed aluminum available at art-supply stores. Paillettes, large sequinlike disks sold in craft stores, may also give the desired effect.

a. With embroidery floss or perle cotton stitch the mirror to the fabric. The grid holds it in place.

b. Stitch another grid diagonally over the first.

c. Placing the needle under the grid patterns, take a small stitch in the fabric, keeping the thread under the needle.

d. Continue buttonhole stitches around the mirror to fill in and cover the grid stitches.

e. Add other embroidery around the shi-sha mirrors if desired.

180

8. Sewing Beads

Here are some ways to attach beads to fabric.

a. Thread a bead on the needle. Sew each bead individually.

b. Thread several beads on a string, lay the string on the fabric, and take a stitch over the thread between each bead.

c. When flat disks are used, bring the thread through the disk, slide a small bead on the needle, and return the needle through the same hole in the disk. The small bead will hold the disk in place. The bead must be slightly larger than the hole in the disk.

d. Flat disks individually stitched through holes look as if they were stacked diagonally on top of each other.

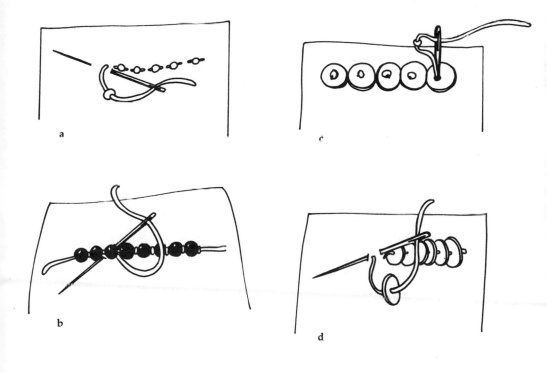

a

c

b

d

9. Pockets

Patch Pockets
Patch pockets can be any shape. Here is how to finish a simple, unlined rectangular or square pocket.
a. Cut out the pocket shape and stitch 1/4" from the top.
b. Turn the top down (1" is adequate) with the right sides of the fabric together and stitch down each side. Clip excess from the corners.
c. Turn the pocket and fold the remaining raw edges to the inside.
d. Pin the pocket to the garment and press. Topstitch around the sides and bottom of the pocket, backstitching on the top edges for reinforcement.

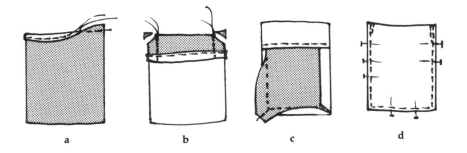

    a   b   c   d

Shaped and/or Lined Pockets
Some pockets need a lining, especially when soft fabrics are used or unusual shapes are desired. Here is how to make a shaped pocket.
a. Cut out a paper pattern the shape of the pocket and add 1/4" on all sides for the seam allowance.
b. Use the pattern to cut out one pocket front and one lining. If the material is soft, interfacing can be used.
c. Placing the right sides of the fabric together, stitch around the edge, leaving a 2" opening for turning. Trim the seams and clip the corners or curves.
d. Turn and press the pocket flat. Slip-stitch the opening closed and sew the pocket to the garment.

a   

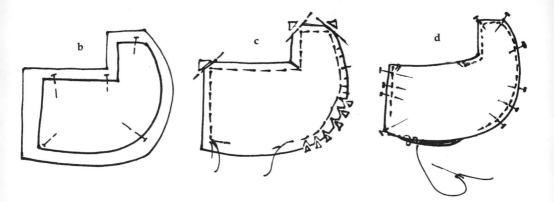

Slit Pockets

Here is how to make inset slit pockets.

a. Cut two pockets.

b. Mark the line for the pocket slit (it should be 2″ shorter than the pocket width).

c. Place right sides of the fabric together. Mark the slit with pins or baste a line.

d. Stitch around the slit 1/4″ from the mark. Clip the corners.

e. Turn and press; topstitch if desired. Pin the back piece to the front pocket and stitch together.

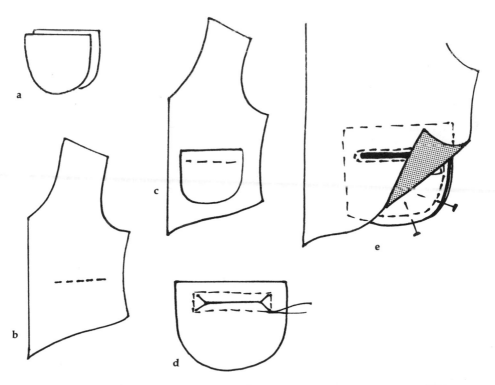

183

Inset Pockets

Here is how to make inset pockets.

a. Cut out two pocket pieces (front and back).

b. Lay one piece on the front of the garment, right sides together, along the seam.

c. Through both thicknesses cut the shape of the desired opening.

d. Stitch around the opening, trim the seam, and clip.

e. Turn back the pocket front and topstitch around the opening if desired.

f. Lay the back piece under the finished pieces, aligning the side seams.

g. Stitch around the pocket from side seam to side seam.

h. Sew the side seams of the garment, treating the pocket and facing as the front surface. Press the seams open.

i. The finished pocket looks like this.

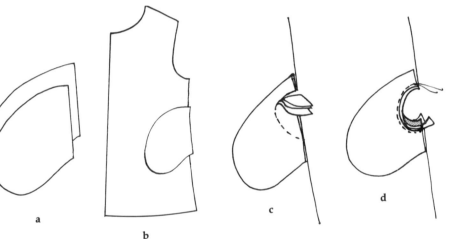

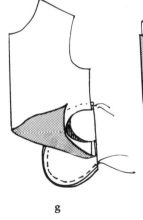

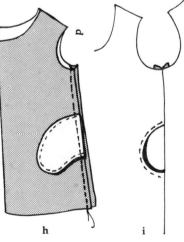

10. Cutwork

Follow this method to do cutwork.

a. Draw a simple design on paper.

b. To transfer the design to the fabric, place dressmaker's carbon (face down) on the right side of the fabric and trace the design with a tracing wheel.

c. Remove papers and machine-stitch around the traced lines on the fabric with contrasting thread.

The design can be finished with a zigzag stitch (by machine) or a buttonhole or satin stitch (by hand). Here is how to do it on the machine.

d. Using a fine stitch and a zigzag setting, stitch over the contrasting lines, creating a finished satin stitch. Practice zigzag stitching on a scrap of fabric until you achieve the desired effect. Here is how to finish by hand.

e. Sew a small running stitch (parallel to the first line) around the entire design.

f. Using a buttonhole (1) or a satin (2) stitch, cover both lines, keeping the stitches very close together.

g. With a sharp scissor cut out the shapes close to the stitching, taking care not to cut the threads.

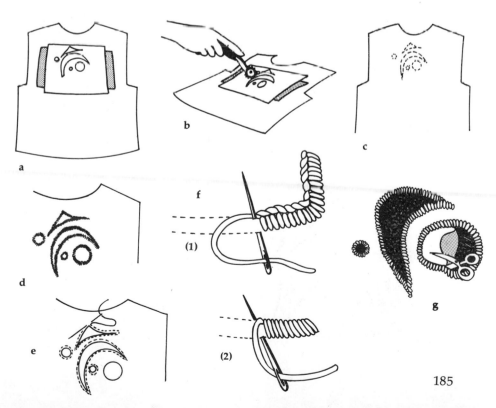

11. Facings

A facing is one way to finish a raw edge—a neck edge, a sleeve or armhole band, a slit pocket, or a hem. Facings usually are stitched in place and turned to the inside of the garment. As a decorative feature they can be made with a contrasting material, and the outer edge cut in any shape, then turned to the outside.

a. Cut the seam edges according to the pattern piece.

b. If you want a shaped outer edge, cut as desired.

c. Place the right side of the facing against the wrong side of the garment.

d. Sew in place, trim, and clip corners or curves. Turn the facing onto the front surface of the garment.

e. Topstitch the outer edges down and press.

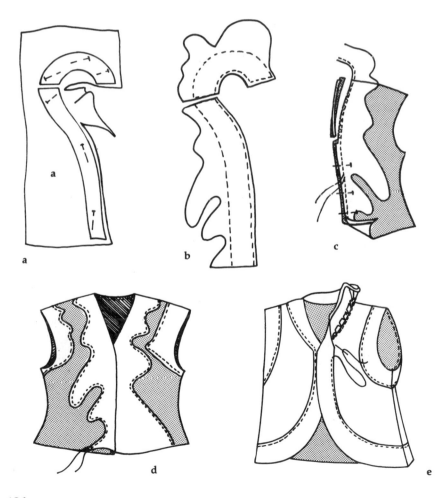

12. Combining Leather and Crochet

To attach crocheted sections to leather, punch holes with a leather punch, awl, or nail. The holes should be 1/4" apart and about 1/4" from the edge of the leather.

a. With a small crochet hook (one that fits in the hole) pull the thread through the hole.

b. Place the yarn over the hook.

c. Pull through the loop.

d. Continue to the next hole.

e. Placing the yarn over, pull through the loop and the first loop.

f. Continue through the remaining holes.

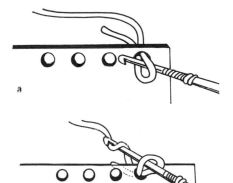

a

d

b

e

c

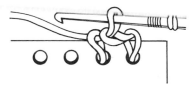

f

13. Tassels

Here is how to make tassels.
a. Wrap the yarn around a piece of cardboard.
b. Tie securely at one end and cut on the opposite end.
c. Wrap thread around the yarn to form a band. Embroider if desired.
d. Stitch a fabric strip around the top and crochet a "cap."

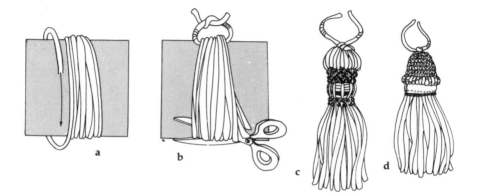

14. Embroidery Stitches

Cretan Stitch

This stitch is very versatile and warrants experimentation—it can be long or short, close or spaced, narrow or wide. To make an open cretan stitch, bring the needle through at (1), keeping the thread above the needle (as on all upward stitches). Insert the needle at (2) and bring it out again at (3). Keep the thread below the needle (as on all downward stitches), insert at (4), and bring out at (5). The shaped or closed cretan stitch is done in the same way as the open cretan.

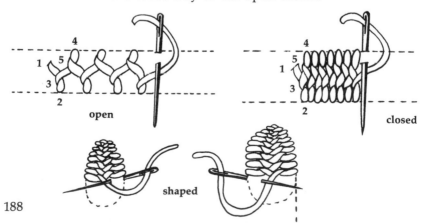

French Knot

Here is how to make a french knot.

a. Bring the thread through the fabric and wind it around the needle three times.

b. Tighten the winds slightly, turn the needle, insert it next to the starting point, and either pull it through to the back or go on to the next knot.

c. This is what a finished french knot looks like.

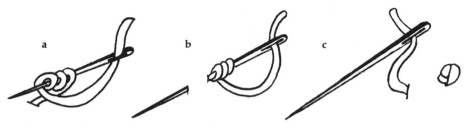

Bullion Knot

Here is how to make a bullion knot.

a. Take a stitch the length desired for the wrapped knot. Leave the needle in the fabric and wrap the thread around the length of the needle.

b. Holding the wraps on the needle with your thumb and forefinger, pull the needle through and tighten.

c. Insert the needle at the starting point and bring the thread to the back, fasten, or go to the next bullion stitch.

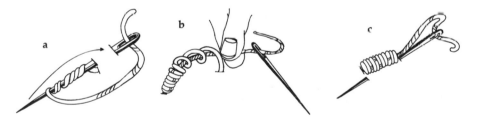

Flystitch

Take a stitch to the side at least 1/4″ wide and leave it slightly loose. Hold the thread down with the thumb. Take a small v-shaped stitch over the center to hold it down. If you are working vertically, start the new stitch directly below the first.

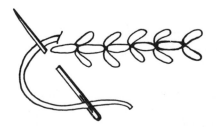

Feather Stitch

Starting at (1), take a stitch 1/4 " to 1/2 " wide to the right (2). Bring the under the needle point (3). Take a stitch to the left and continue.

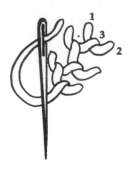

Satin Stitch

Satin stitches are straight stitches that are used to fill in a shape. If the space is wide, the stitches can be made slightly shorter so that two will be needed to fill the width. For a padded effect several rows of running or chain stitches may be worked underneath the satin stitch.

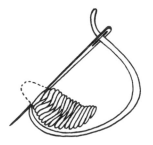

Chain Stitch

a. To make a closed chain stitch, starting at (1), bring the thread up, and hold down with your thumb. Insert the needle at (1) again and bring the point out a small stitch away, keeping the thread under the needle point. Pull the thread through.

b. The open chain stitch is a good stitch to use when the widths of stitching vary. Start at (1). Hold the stitch down with your thumb, insert the needle at (2), bring the point out at (3), and leave the loop loose. Insert the needle at (4), keeping the thread under the needle point.

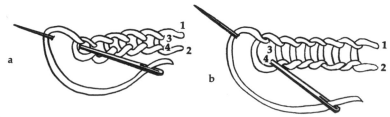

190

Vandyke Stitch

This stitch gives a nice braid effect. Start at (1) and take a small stitch at (2) from right to left. Insert the needle at (3) and come out at (4). Without putting the point into the fabric put the needle under the cross of the previous stitch at (2) from right to left and insert at (5). Continue in the same manner.

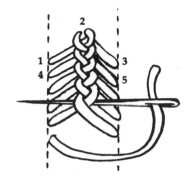

Backstitch

Bring the thread through on the stitch line (real or imagined) and take a small stitch backward through the fabric. Bring the needle point up through the fabric slightly in front of the previous stitch and continue in the same way.

Couching

Lay a piece of thread, string, yarn, fabric, or leather along the design line. Baste or pin the line first if desired. With another thread fasten with small, evenly spaced stitches.

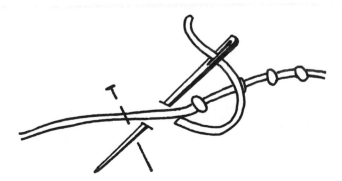

15. *Faggoting*

Faggoting is a decorative method of fastening two pieces of material together. These pieces should be finished—hemmed, faced, or lined. Swedish knot is one stitch used for faggoting; other stitches to try include buttonhole, feather, or cretan stitch.

16. *Smocking*

Smocking is a means of adding fullness, elasticity, and decoration to a plain garment. Simple embroidery stitches hold the gather in place. Add 5 ″ or 6 ″ to the pattern piece that you wish to smock. The fabric should be quite firm—denim, poplin, or another heavy, tightly woven fabric. Make sure that the pieces are cut on the straight of grain.

a. Baste lines 3/8″ apart with 3/8″-long stitches. Make sure that you have enough thread on the needle to complete the horizontal row.

b. Knot the thread securely. Baste as above, leaving the thread unfastened at the end of the row. It is used to pull up the gathering stitches.

c. Pull gathers firmly and tie the loose thread ends tightly in a knot.

d. Embroider on the front face of the gathers to hold them in place. The embroidery stitches can be very simple, such as chain, feather, or backstitch.

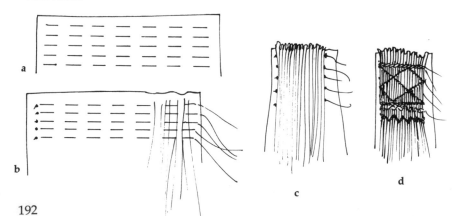

17. Patchwork

Patchwork is a good method to make colorful sections of garments from recycled scraps of old clothing. Wash the pieces to preshrink them and to remove sizing.

a. Cut out pieces for patchwork.

b. Stitch them together, using 1/4″ seams. Stitching row by row is easiest, but you can also work from the center of the motif out to the edge and then sew the motifs together. A small stitch (10 to 12 per inch) and a straight line are two important rules for successful patchwork. If an intricate pattern is preferred, you might want to make a paper template first and to cut the pieces from it, leaving a 1/4″ seam allowance.

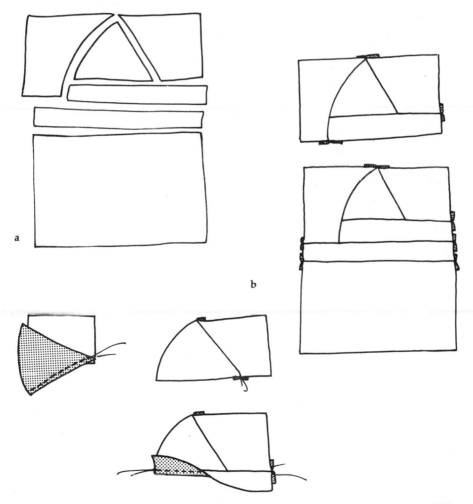

c. Press all seams open.

d. Cut out the garment, using the pieced fabric that you have made.

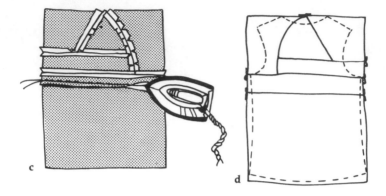

c

d

Strip patchwork can be very effective and easy. The strips are sewn to a backing so that the fabric or pattern sections are lined in the same step.

e. Cut strips of fabric, preferably 3/4" to 2" wide.

f. Sew pieces of fabric into long strips and press to one side.

g. Lay the pieced strip on the fabric, right sides together, starting from one side or the middle.

h. Fold back to the right side and pin close to the stitched seam. Continue with the next strip. If a special design is preferred rather than a random pattern, draw the design on the background material and follow it when cutting the strips. To make a quilted jacket with the strip method, baste a layer of polyester batting to the lining and proceed as above.

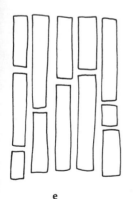

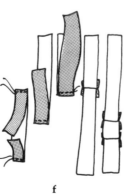

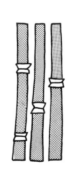

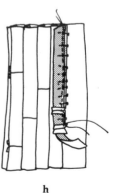

e

f

g

h

18. Reverse Applique

Here is how to do reverse appliqué.

a. Stack layers of various-colored fabrics on top of each other—cottons or cotton blends work well.

b. Place dressmaker's carbon face down on top of the design. Trace around the shapes with a tracing wheel.

c. Baste around the shapes 1/2" from the edge.

d. Cut through the layers to expose the chosen color. Turn under the raw edge and blind-stitch in place.

e. The finished shape looks like this.

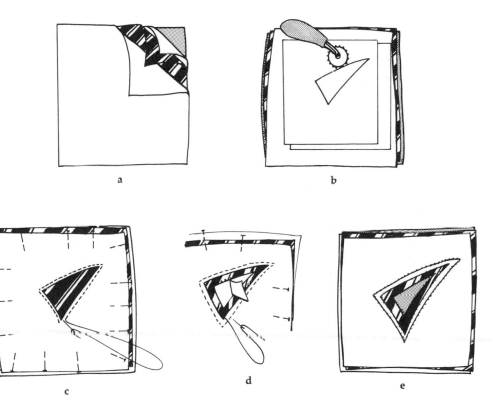

a

b

c

d

e

19. *Trapunto*

Trapunto is a form of quilting. The design is a bas relief—it is stuffed or corded to stand out.

a. The design is traced onto thin cotton (such as batiste), which is used as the backing.

b. Baste this backing to the wrong side of the fabric.

c. Stitch over the lines of the design through both layers of fabric, using a small stitch on the machine or sewing by hand.

d. When the stitching is finished, pad the sections with wool yarn threaded on a blunt needle. Pass the needle through the backing where necessary.

e. If the design motif has large shapes, the backing can be slit, wool (or quilt batting) stuffed into the section, and the slit whipped together.

f. The finished trapunto design looks like this.

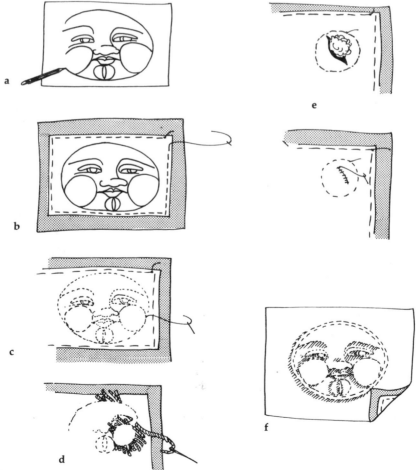

20. Quilting

Quilting is a textile technique that is especially suitable for unusual and warm garments. It can be combined with patchwork, appliqué, or plain material with a filler and lining to make very individual fabrics. If the top layer is patchwork or appliqué, the design can be emphasized by quilting around it. If you are using plain fabrics and wish the quilted lines to form the design, draw the desired design on tissue paper. Place the paper on top of the fabric and, using a soft pencil, puncture the paper to make dots on the fabric. You can also use dressmaker's carbon and a tracing wheel. Pencil lines can be made around templates of cardboard, plastic, or sandpaper (which won't slip).

a. Cut pattern pieces out of the fabric and lining. The main pieces of the garment may be sewn together at this point, or each piece may be quilted first and finished later.

b. Lay the lining on a flat surface and cover with a *thin* layer of filler, with the fabric on top. As a filler bonded polyester batting is lightweight, does not mat, and washes easily. Divide it in half or thinner, as preferred. Other suggested fillers are sections of old wool blankets (thin) or prewashed flannel or terrycloth.

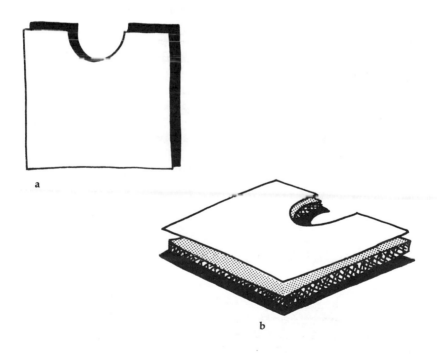

a

b

c. Baste lines in rows about 6" to 8" apart to keep the three layers together.

d. If desired, use a quilting hoop or thumbtack the layers to a wood frame such as a canvas stretcher (available at art-supply stores). In either case start in the center to ensure that the work is kept flat. Following the pencil marks, make small running stitches, using Dacron-covered thread or 80 quilting thread and a short, sharp needle (#8 or #9).

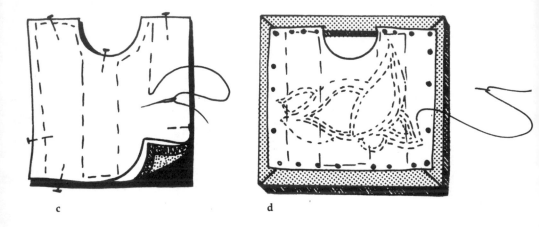

c   d

Tufted or hand-tied quilting is another method for making a quilted garment. It is faster than stitching, and the ties can be arranged in a decorative pattern. The preliminary steps (a and b above) are the same as for the previous method. Step (c) is optional; pinning the layers together works just as well.

e. Mark a dot, using a pencil and a ruler, every 3" or 4" to indicate where the ties should be placed. Using a sharp yarn needle and doubled wool yarn, insert the needle on the dot through all three layers. Leave about 2" of yarn on top and come back 1/4" away on the top layer.

f, g. Tie a square knot (right over left, then left over right) and cut the yarn, leaving 1" of thread. Continue. The knots can be made on either side of the garment, depending on the effect desired. When all the stitching or tying is finished, bias-bind the edges and finish the garment.

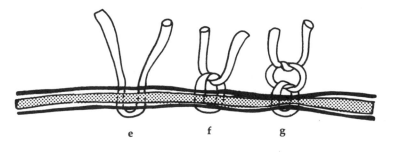

e   f   g

21. Stenciling

Supplies
a. Fabrics: most natural fibers and blends take paint well—consult paint manufacturer's suggestions.
b. Small commercial knife (such as X-acto) or single-edge blade
c. Stencil paper (available at hobby stores)
d. Stenciling brush or round, stiff bristle brush—all bristles must be the same length
e. Flat glass or plate surface to mix paint
f. Water-soluble fabric paint (see the list of suppliers)

Method
a. Draw the design on the stencil paper.
b. Cut out with a sharp knife or razor blade.

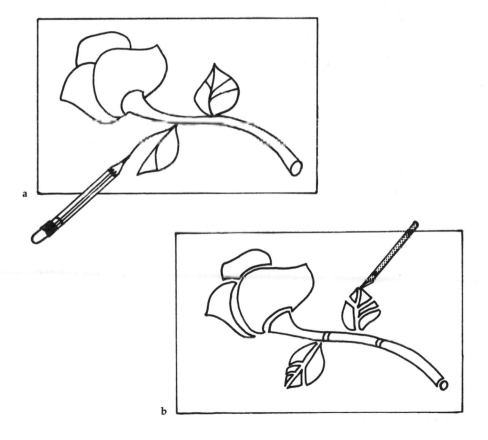

a

b

c. Fasten the material to be painted with masking tape if it is firm—this is probably not necessary.

d. Choose colors and mix them on glass. Use *very* little paint on the brush.

e. Put the stencil on the fabric, using masking tape to secure the paper. Paint with a stippling technique (up-and-down motion). If several colors are used on one design, masking tape may be used to cover the spaces not in use, or separate stencils can be cut for each color. In either case it is best not to remove the stencil until you have stippled the entire design. Wipe the stencil clean with a wet sponge. Rinse the brush in water. Let paint dry several hours and press with a moderately hot iron (relative to the fabric) to set the colors.

f. The stenciled fabric can now be cut out and sewn into unique garments.

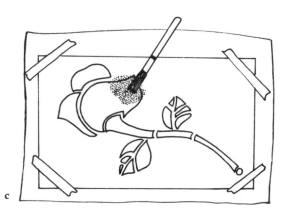

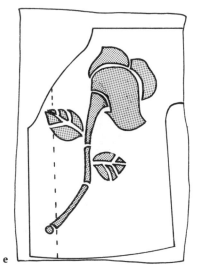

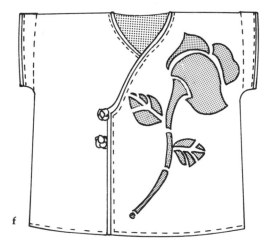

22. Pin Weaving

Pin weaving is one of the most versatile weaving methods, because any shape is possible. As a base for the weaving use a heavy cardboard, a cardboard box, or fiberboard. It is best to make a paper pattern. Either draw the design on a piece of cardboard or lay the pattern down and pin it in place.

a. The straight pins used to fasten the warp are placed at a very low angle to the cardboard. They should be set 1/8" to 1/4" apart. When using fine weft threads in a detailed design, the warps should be close together. For larger wefts consider a wider spacing.

b. Make an open slip knot and fasten it to the first pin. It is best to insert the pins as the warping progresses. When the entire pattern shape has been warped, fasten the warp thread to the last pin with an open slip knot.

a

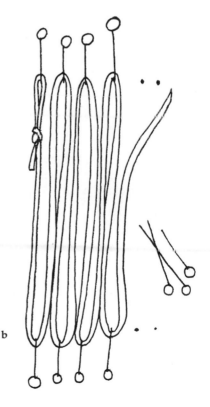

b

c. If the warp is to show, use a single or a thin thread. If the warp is to be completely covered, use a doubled or thick yarn. Thread the yarn needle and start weaving over and under the threads. Start a new thread 1" or 2" in from the edge of the warp, continue weaving to the edge, and return. This assures a smooth selvage. The first and last row next to the pins must be woven very carefully. The needle and thread must pass *between* warp threads on each pin. It is wise to weave the ends by the pins first.

d. The weft should be packed firmly. The tool commonly used for this purpose is called a beater, but a table fork or comb can also be used. To keep the edges of the weaving straight, "bubble" the weft as it is inserted. This also makes the warp easier to cover completely. As the filler is woven across, lay it in rather loosely in an arc, make several smaller arcs, and beat with the beater. When the weaving is completed, remove the pins—the pin weaving needs no further work—no warp ends to tie or weave in. This completed piece may be appliquéd, lined, or embroidered to fabric.

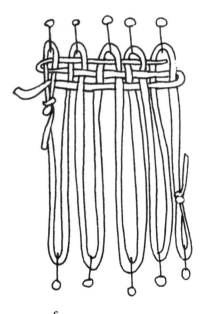

c

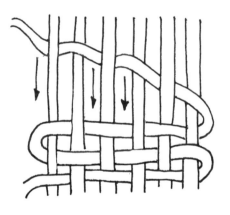

d

23. Weaving into Fabric

This technique can be used to make designs for yokes, insets, sleeve bands, or any other purpose.

a. Cut slits 1/4" to 3/8" wide in the fabric (for the warp).

b. Pin the fabric securely to cardboard.

c. Weave with yarn and/or fabric strips (narrow).

d. Line the woven piece with an extra piece of fabric to keep it firm. Finish the garment. Don't be concerned about raveling—it adds dimension and wears well.

a

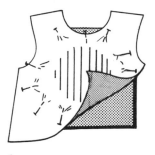

b

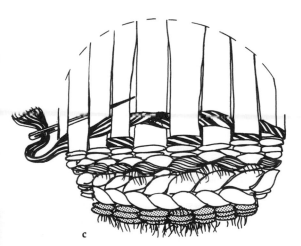

c

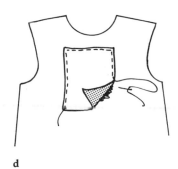

d

BIBLIOGRAPHY

Costumes
Baskt, Leon, *The Decorative Art of Leon Baskt*, Dover, 1972
Blum, Stella, *Designs by Erté*, Dover, 1972
Braun and Schneider, *Historic Costume in Pictures*, Dover, 1975
Burnham, Dorothy, *Cut My Cote*, Royal Ontario Museum, 1973
Fairservis, Walter A., *Costumes of the East*, Chatham Press, 1971
Funaro, Diane, *The Yestermorrow Clothes Book*, Chilton, 1976
Hartley, Dorothy, *Mediaeval Costume and Life*, Scribner's, 1931
Rubens, Alfred, *The History of Jewish Costume*, Crown, 1967
Selbie, Robert, *The Anatomy of Costume*, Crescent, 1977
Tilke, Max, *Costume Patterns and Designs*, Hastings House, 1974
Yarwood, Doreen, *European Costume*, Larousse, 1975

Design and Technique
Day, JoAnne C., *Art Nouveau, Cut and Use Stencils*, Dover, 1977
Day, JoAnne C., *The Complete Book of Stencilcraft*, Simon & Schuster, 1974
Dendel, Esther Warner, *African Fabric Crafts*, Taplinger, 1974
D'Harcourt, Raoul, *Textiles of Ancient Peru*, University of Washington, 1962
Ericson, Lois and Diane, *The Bag Book*, Van Nostrand Reinhold, 1976
Frew, Hannah, *Three-Dimensional Embroidery*, Van Nostrand Reinhold, 1975
Kafka, Frances J., *Batik, Tie-Dyeing, Stenciling, Silk Screen, Block Printing*, Dover, 1973
Lubell, Cecil, *Textile Collections of the World*, vols. 1 (United States and Canada), 2 (United Kingdom and Ireland), 3 (France), Van Nostrand Reinhold, 1976, 1977
MacKenzie, Clinton, *New Deisgn in Crochet*, Van Nostrand Reinhold, 1972
Matsuya, *Japanese Design Motifs*, Dover, 1972
Meilach, Dona and Hinz, *How to Create Your Own Designs*, Doubleday, 1975
Menten, Theodore, *Art Deco, Cut and Use Stencils*, Dover, 1977
Willcox, Donald, *New Design in Stitchery*, Van Nostrand Reinhold, 1970
Williams, Geoffrey, *African Designs*, Dover, 1971

DESIGNERS

B. J. Adams
2821 Arizona Terrace, N.W.
Washington, D.C. 20016

Betty Auchard
115 Belhaven Drive
Los Gatos, California 95030

Kristine Barrett
624 N. 12th Street
Pocatello, Idaho 83201

Berta Bray
Box 356
El Grananda, California 94018

Enola Dickey
Box 133
Amador City, California 95601

Jo Diggs
RFD 3, Bassett Road, Box 426
Winslow, Maine 04902

Linda Edison
237 N. Pine Street
Orange, California 92666

Lois Ericson
Box 349
Tahoe City, California 95730

Diane Ericson Frode
20250 Wilder Ct.
Prunedale, California 93907

Nancy Gano
1482 Marcia Avenue
San Jose, California 95125

Pat Goldstene
1214 Bucknell Drive
Davis, California 95616

Susan Grant
P.O. Box 126
Caliton, New Jersey 07830

Jean M. Hudson
12572 Woodland Lane
Garden Grove, California 92640

Heidi Hybl
Grimes Ranch
Palo Colorado Canyon
Monterey, California 93940

Rebecca Yamaguchi Kanow
31 Harvest Street
Salinas, California 93901

Perri Kimono
2130 Fell Street, #5
San Francisco, California 94117

Nancy Kathleen Love
2147 Russell Street
Berkeley, California 94705

Nancy MacLeod
455 Hudson
Oakland, California 94618

Pamela Magnuson
336 J Street, #25
Davis, California 95616

Colleen M. Miner
P.O. Box 1664
Tahoe City, California 95730

Suzanne Ness O'Curry
c/o 1547 Grand
Astoria, Oregon 97103

Nancy Papa
121 Stacia Street
Los Gatos, California 95030

Alix E. Peshette
8622 Pershing Avenue
Fair Oaks, California 95628

Anna V.A. Polesny
149 Leroy Street
Binghamton, New York 1390

Joanne Purpus
c/o Palos Verdes Art Center
5504 Crestridge
Rancho Palos Verdes, California 90279

Marcia Reed
5404 Coral Reef Avenue
La Jolla, California 92037

Dorie Riley
1961 Ren Circle
Tustin, California 92680

Diane Ritch
5425 Entrance Drive
Soquel, California 95073

Cindy Van Dine
P.O. Box 8942
Aspen, Colorado 81611

Salley Voss
18578 Cottonwood Street
Fountain Valley, California 92708

P.J. Walton
15305 Callahan Rd.
Reno, Navada 89511

Annabel Woodsmall
c/o Casa De Las Tejedoras
1619 E. Edinger
Santa Ana, California 92705

Andrea Woynick
30626 Hennepin
Garden City, Michigan 48135

SUPPLIERS

Berkeley Arts
2590 Durant Avenue
Berkeley, California 94704
Versatex paint for textiles, Inko dyes, batik
  supplies

Big Dogma
1551 Solano Avenue
Albany, California 94706
Beads and oriental artifacts

Fiber Arts (bimonthly magazine)
3717 4th Street N.W.
Albuquerque, New Mexico 87107

vear
x 98
Forestville, California 95436
Ethnic patterns

Handweavers of Los Altos
393 State Street
Los Altos, California 94022
Shi-sha mirrors, antler buttons, yarns

Kasuri Dyeworks
1959 Shattuck Avenue
Berkeley, California 94704
Japanese fabrics, supplies for paste resist
  printing

Las Manos
12215 Coit Road
Dallas, Texas 75251
Weaving supplies, beads

Natalie's
Clifton Park Plaza
Mechanicville, New York 12118
English peasant smocks

Nance O'Banion and Cindy Sägen
Fiberworks
1940 Bonita
Berkeley, California 94704
Fiberfinder (a guide to Bay Area sources)

Poppy
2072 Addison Street
Berkeley, California 94704
Imported fabrics

Yvonne Porcella
3619 Shoemake
Modesto, California 95351
Five Ethnic Patterns

Raye's Eclectic Craft Yarns
8157 Commercial Street
La Mesa, California 92041
Yarn, beads, shi-sha mirrors (wholesale
  only)

Screen Process Supplies
1199 E. 12
Oakland, California 94606
Inko dye (heat-set dye)

Someplace
2990 Adeline Street
Berkeley, California 94703
Lace, beads

Straw into Gold
5533 College Avenue
Oakland, California 94618
Fibers, dyes, trims, buttons, Japanese embroidery thread

Thai Silk
253 State Street
Los Altos, California 94022
Imported silks

The Shop
Box 133
Amador City, California 95601
Yarn and custom-handwoven fabrics

The Toy Works
Middle Falls, New York
Printed toys to stuff

Nancy Welsh
2 Fair Oaks Lane
Atherton, California 94025
Tassels (booklet)

Wezelman, Dick and Beany
1750 Capistrano Street
Berkeley, California 94707
African textiles, yardage, beads

Yarn and Weaver's Things
1250 Howe Avenue
Sacramento, California

Yone's Beads
478 Union Street
San Francisco, California 94133

INDEX